Handwriting Without Tears®
by Learning Without Tears

Name:

Try the new Digital Student App! Students can complete assignments, access letter formation tools, and work from home or school.

hwt-student.lwtears.com

Cursive Handwriting

pianist   teacher   singer

LEARNING
Without Tears®

8001 MacArthur Blvd
Cabin John, MD 20818
LWTears.com | 888.983.8409

Author: Jan Z. Olsen, OTR
Content Advisors: Christina Bretz, MS, OTR/L, Tania Ferrandino, OTR/L
Illustrators: Jan Z. Olsen, OTR, Julie Koborg
Graphic Designers: Carol Johnston, Julie Koborg
Editors: Annie Cassidy, Megan Parker

Copyright © 2022 Learning Without Tears
Tenth Edition
ISBN: 978-1-952970-80-1
123456789BRB242322
Printed in the USA

The contents of this consumable workbook are protected by US copyright law. If a workbook has been purchased for a child, the author and Learning Without Tears give limited permission to copy pages for additional practice or homework for that child. No copied pages from this book can be given to another person without written permission from Learning Without Tears.

January 2, 2022

Dear Student,
    Can you read this?
It's cursive. Your teacher will help you learn to read and write cursive. I hope that you enjoy the book.

Sincerely,
Jan Z. Olsen

Aa	Bb	Cc	Dd	Ee	Ff	Gg	Hh	Ii	Jj	Kk	Ll	Mm
9	50	8	10	20	24	12	14	32	34	38	22	60

TABLE OF CONTENTS

Preparing for Cursive

Letter to Students 1
Table of Contents 2–3
Cursive Lowercase & Capitals 4
Cursive Warm-Ups & Name 5
Paper Placement & Pencil Skills 6
Learn & Check 7

Lowercase Letters
Magic c Letters

c 8
a 9
d 10–11
g 12–13

Lowercase: h t p

h 14–15
t 16–17
p 18–19

Lowercase: e l f

e 20–21
l 22–23
f 24–25
  Review & Mastery 26–27

Lowercase: u y i j

u 28–29
y 30–31
i 32–33
j 34–35
  Review & Mastery 36–37

Lowercase: k r s

k 38–39
r 40–41
s 42–43
  Review & Mastery 44–45

Tow Truck Letters: o w b v

o 46–47
w 48–49
b 50–51
v 52–53

Tricky Connections: after o + w 54–55
Tricky Connections: after b + v 56–57
  Review & Mastery 58–59

Nn	Oo	Pp	Qq	Rr	Ss	Tt	Uu	Vv	Ww	Xx	Yy	Zz
62	46	18	68	40	42	16	28	52	48	66	30	69

Lowercase: m m

m 60–61
m 62–63
Special Situation m 64
Special Situation n 65

Lowercase: x q z

x 66–67
q 68
z 69
    Review & Mastery 70–71

Capitals

A B C D E F 72
G H I J K L M 73
N O P Q R S T 74
U V W X Y Z 75
    Capital Connections & Review 76

Writing Activities

Poem - "You're or Your?" 77
Words - Greek & Latin 78
Paragraph - Maps 79
Punctuation - Dates, Greetings & Closings 80
Friendly Letter - Thank You 81
Words - Suffixes 82
Paragraph - Galileo 83
Symbols - Keyboard 84
Letters - Silent Letters k, w & b 85
Sentences - Capital Rules 86
Names - Musicians 87
Paragraph - Tropical Rainforest 88
Sentences - Capitalization 89
Paragraph - Garrett Morgan, Sr. 90
Words - Compound Words 91
Paragraph - Bathysphere 92
Paragraph - Ocean 93
Sentences - Quotations 94

Cursive Lowercase

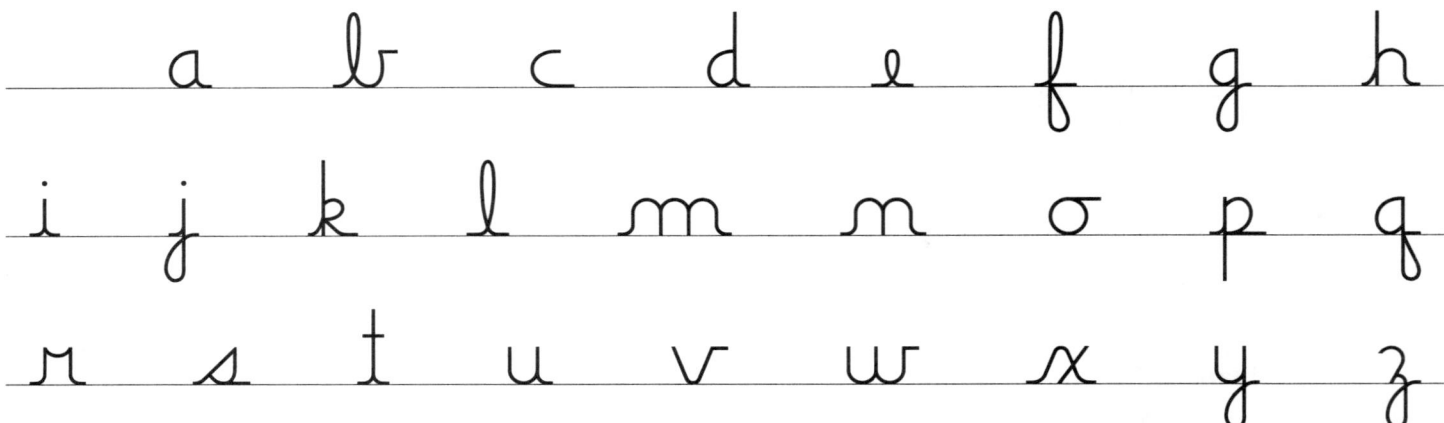

Connection Rule: When two letters are connected, the first letter is the "boss" of the connection.
1. Base line connections: If the first letter ends on the base line (22 letters), start the next letter on the base line.
2. High connections: If the first letter ends high (Tow Truck Letters: o, w, b, v), start the next letter high.

Cursive Capitals

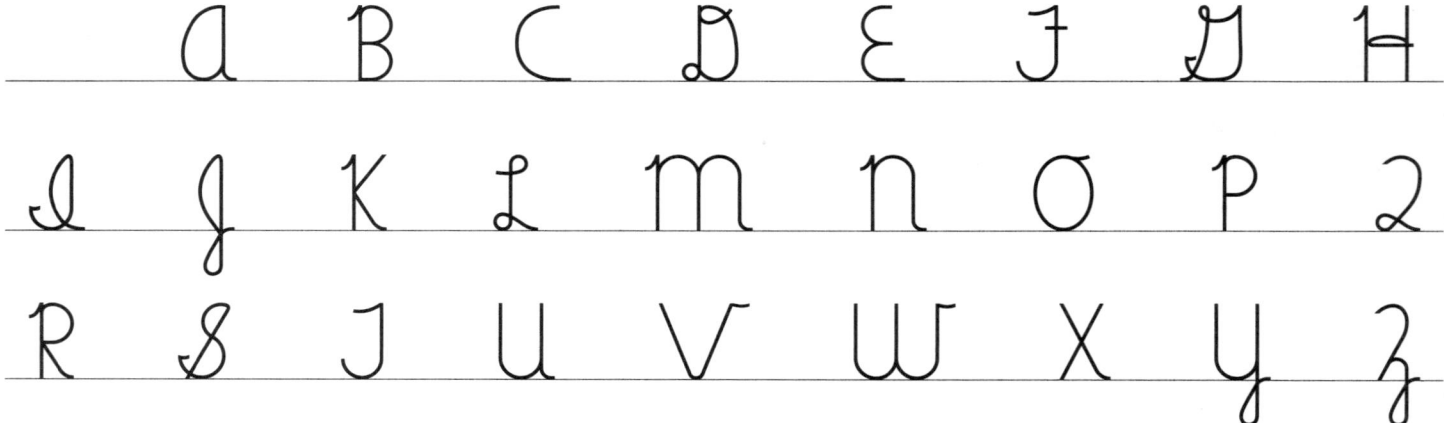

Connection Rule: Capitals do not have to connect.
1. Connect if it's easy; the capital ends on the base line and on the right side.
2. Don't connect if it's tricky, a high ending, or wrong side.

Cursive Warm-Ups

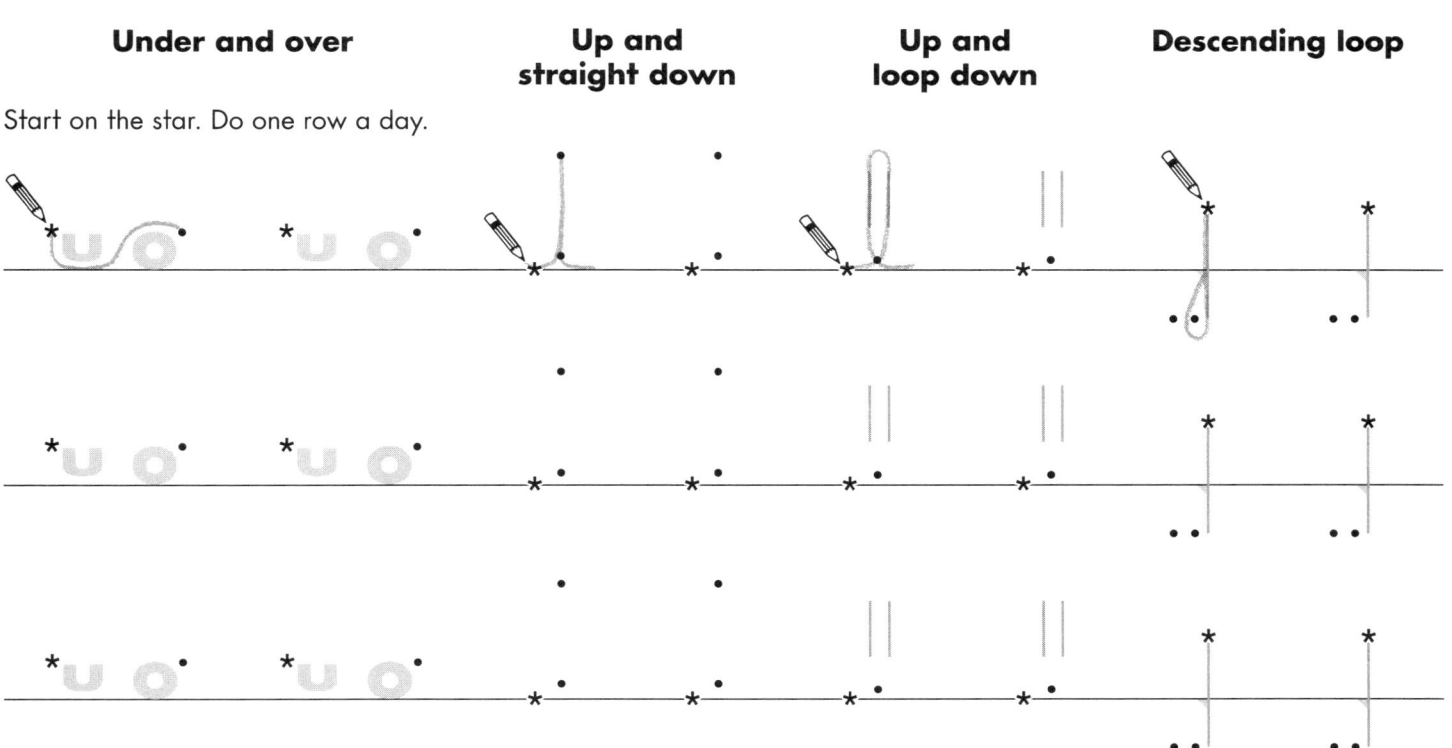

My Name in Cursive

Name:

Name:

Paper Placement & Pencil Skills

LEFT-HANDED
Place the **left** corner higher.

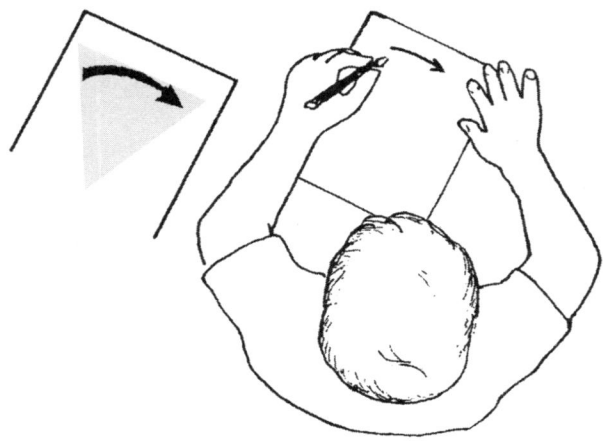

RIGHT-HANDED
Place the **right** corner higher.

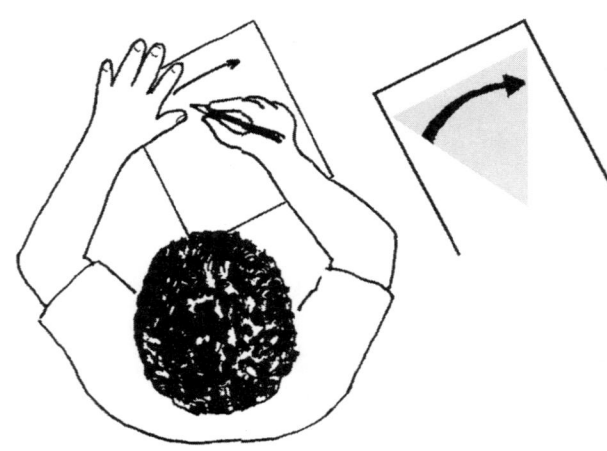

Standard grip: Hold pencil with **thumb + index finger.** Pencil rests on middle finger.

Eraser points to **left** shoulder.

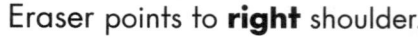

Eraser points to **right** shoulder.

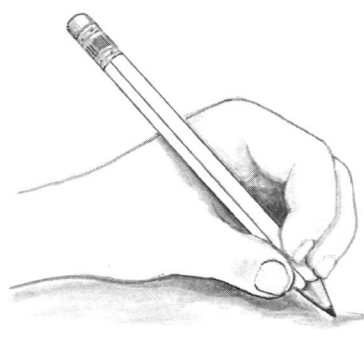

Alternate grip: Hold pencil with **thumb + index and middle fingers.** Pencil rests on ring finger.

Learn & Check

Learn letters, words, sentences, and how to check them.
When you see the box , it's time to check your work.

 **Check letter** Teachers: Help children ☑ their letter for correct start, steps, and bump.

1. Start correctly.   **2.** Do each step.   **3.** Bump the lines.

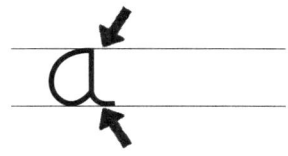

 Check word Teachers: Help children ☑ their word for correct letter size, placement, and Connections.

1. Make letters the correct size.
2. Place letters correctly: tall, small, or descending.

3. Connect letters correctly.

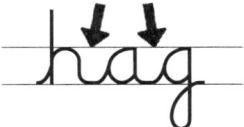

Tall   **Small**   **Descending**

 **Check sentence** Teachers: Help children ☑ their sentence for correct capitalization, word spacing, and ending punctuation.

1. Start with a capital.   **2.** Put space between words.   **3.** End with **.** **?** or **!**

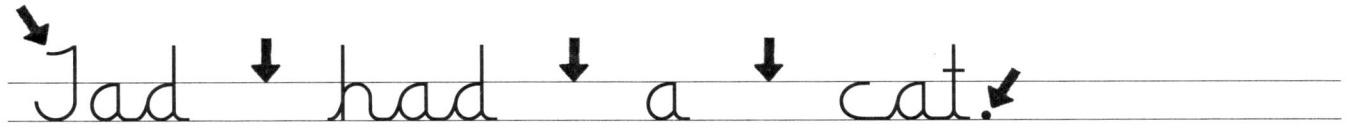

© 2022 Learning Without Tears   Cursive Handwriting

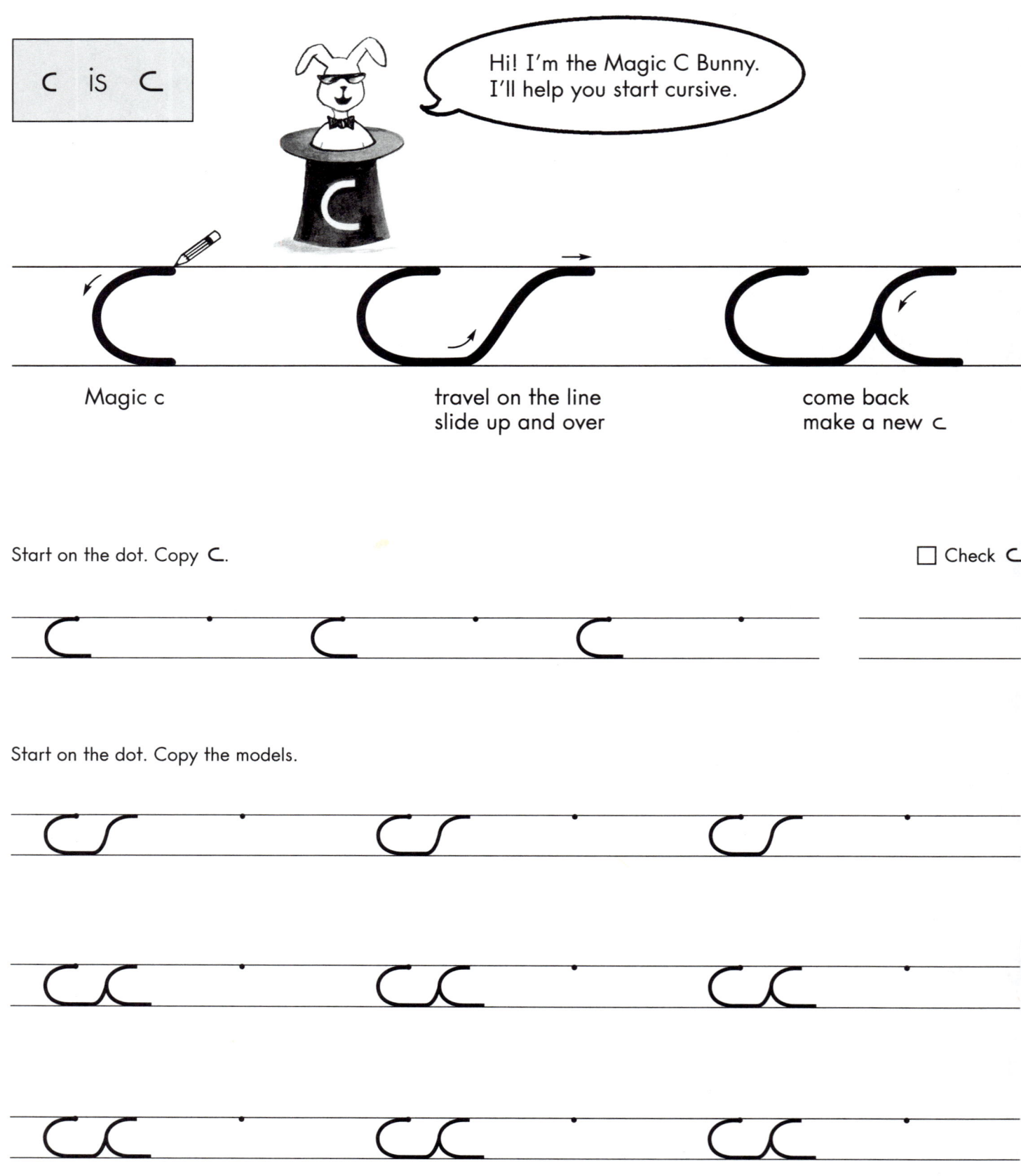

a is a

Change c into a. Here's how:

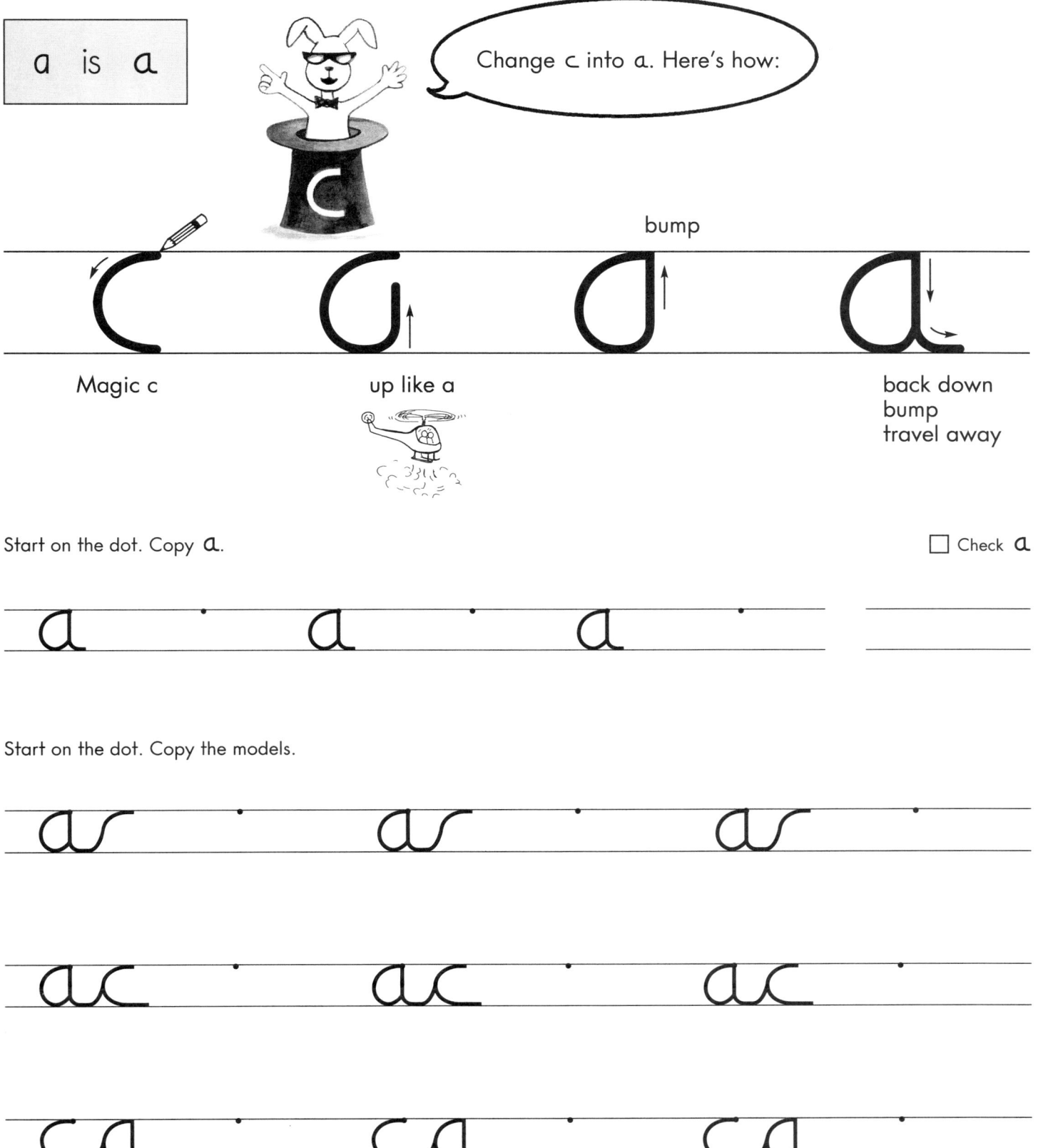

Magic c — up like a — bump — back down bump travel away

Start on the dot. Copy a. ☐ Check a

Start on the dot. Copy the models.

Cursive Handwriting

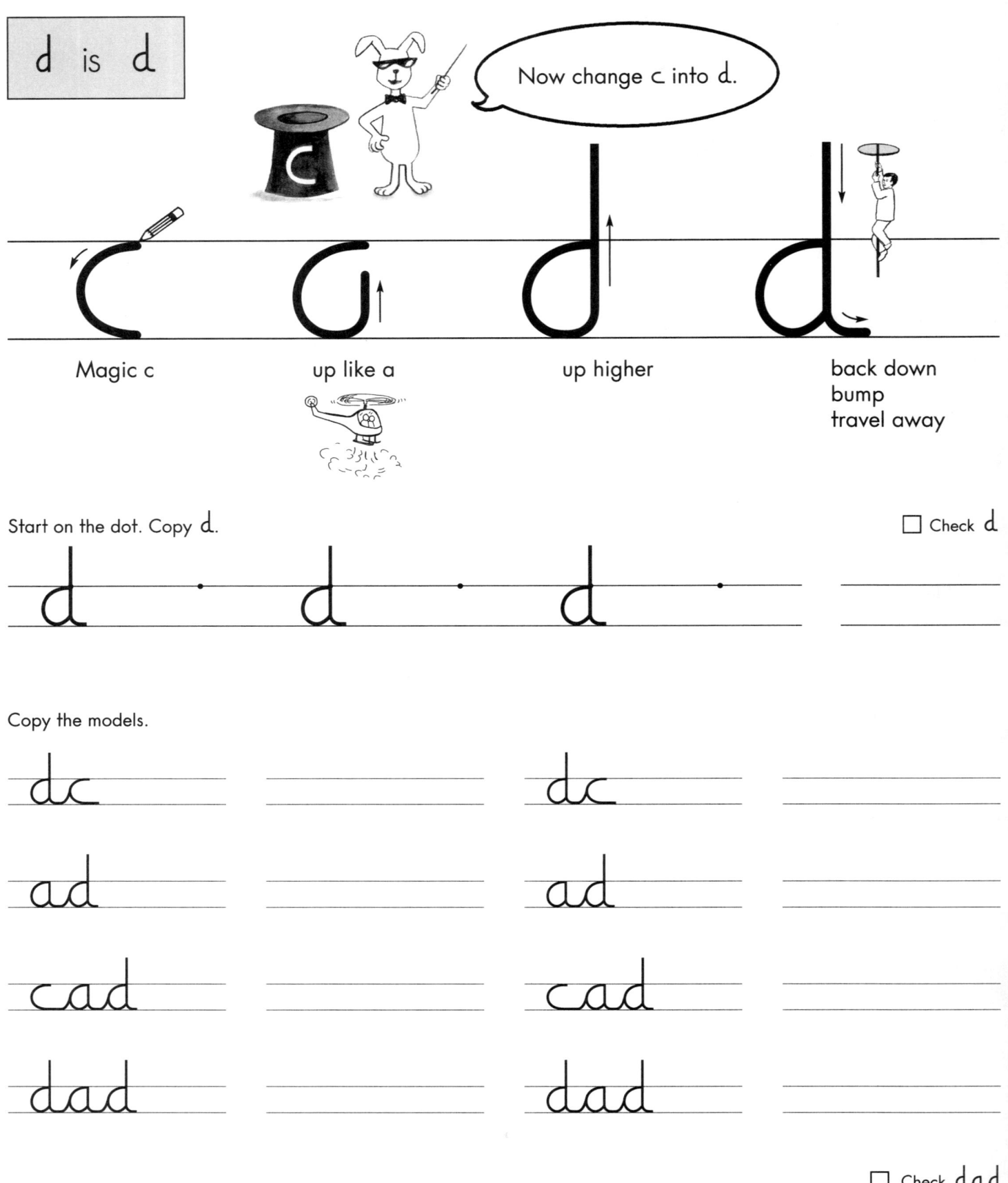

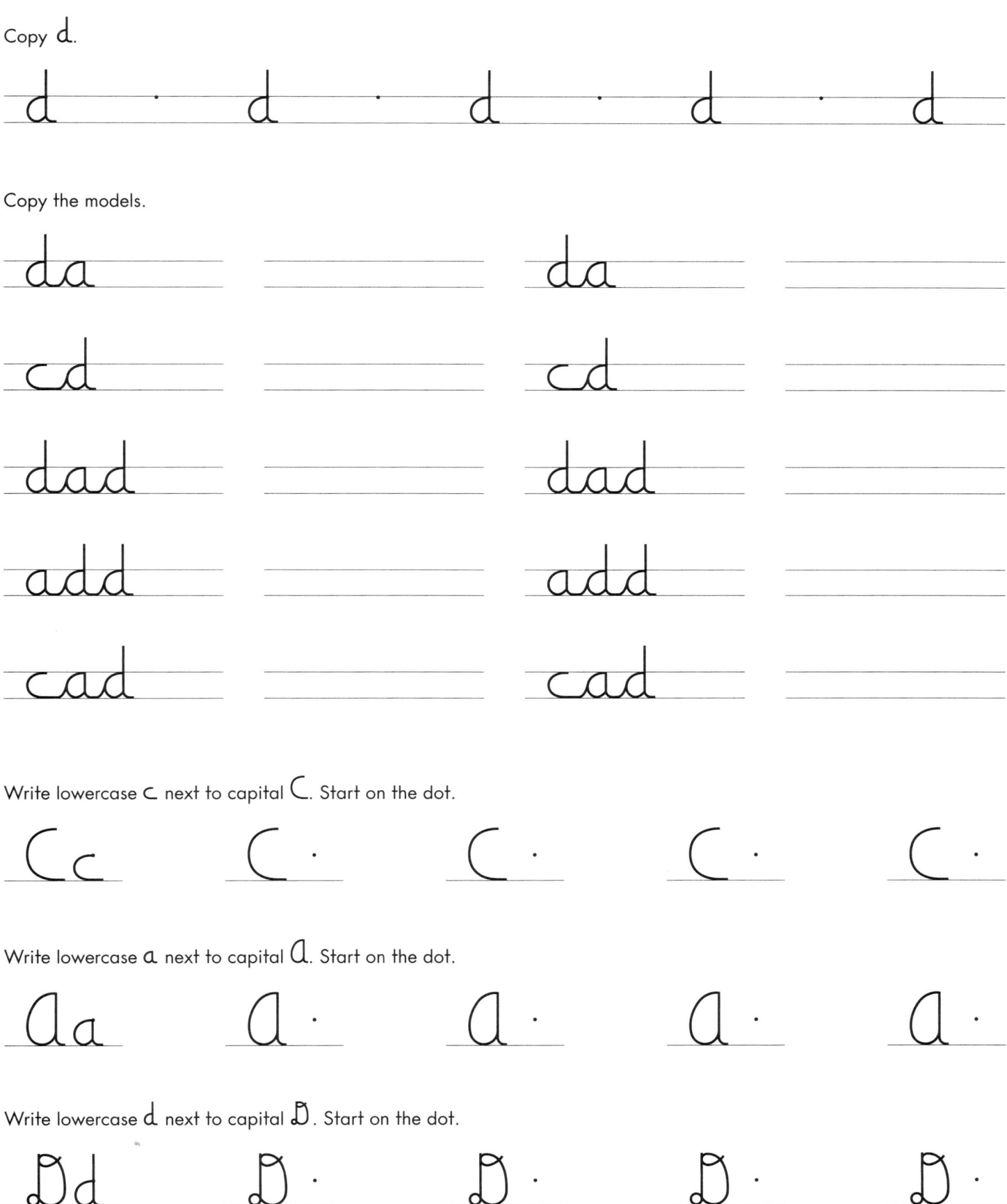

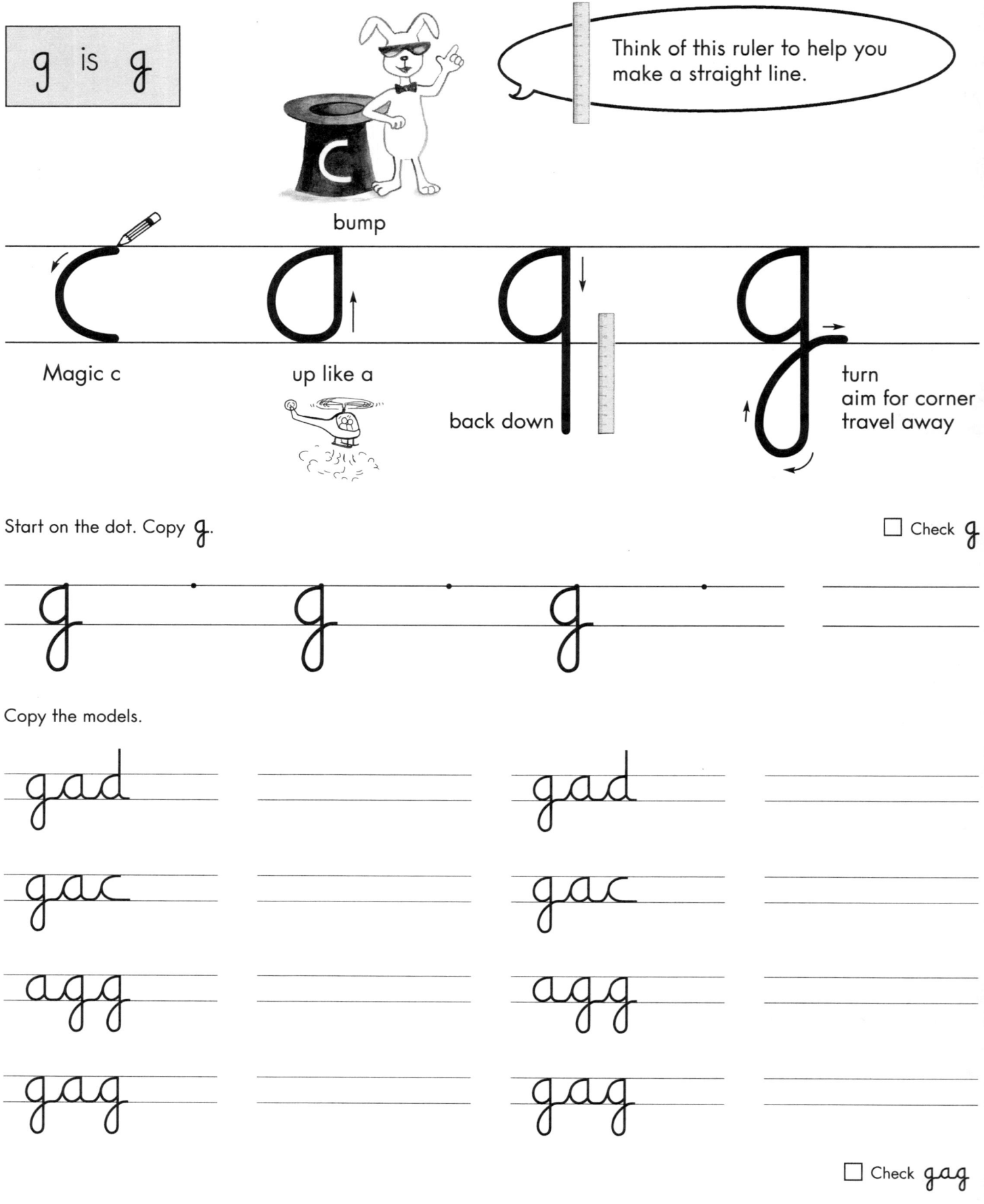

Copy g.

Copy the models.

gc

ga

gg

ag

gag

gac

gad

Write lowercase g next to capital G. Start on the dot.

Gg   G.   G.   G.   G.

© 2022 Learning Without Tears · Cursive Handwriting · **13**

h is h

travel
up like a

back down
bump

climb back up
and over

and down
bump
travel away

Can you climb up + over + down?

Start on the dot. Copy h. ☐ Check h

h .   h .   h .

Copy the models.

gh   gh
hag   hag
cha   cha
had   had

☐ Check had

14 Cursive Handwriting   © 2022 Learning Without Tears

Copy h.

Copy the models.

ha		ha	
ah		ah	
had		had	
cha		cha	
hag		hag	
hac		hac	
aha		aha	

Write lowercase h next to capital H. Start on the dot.

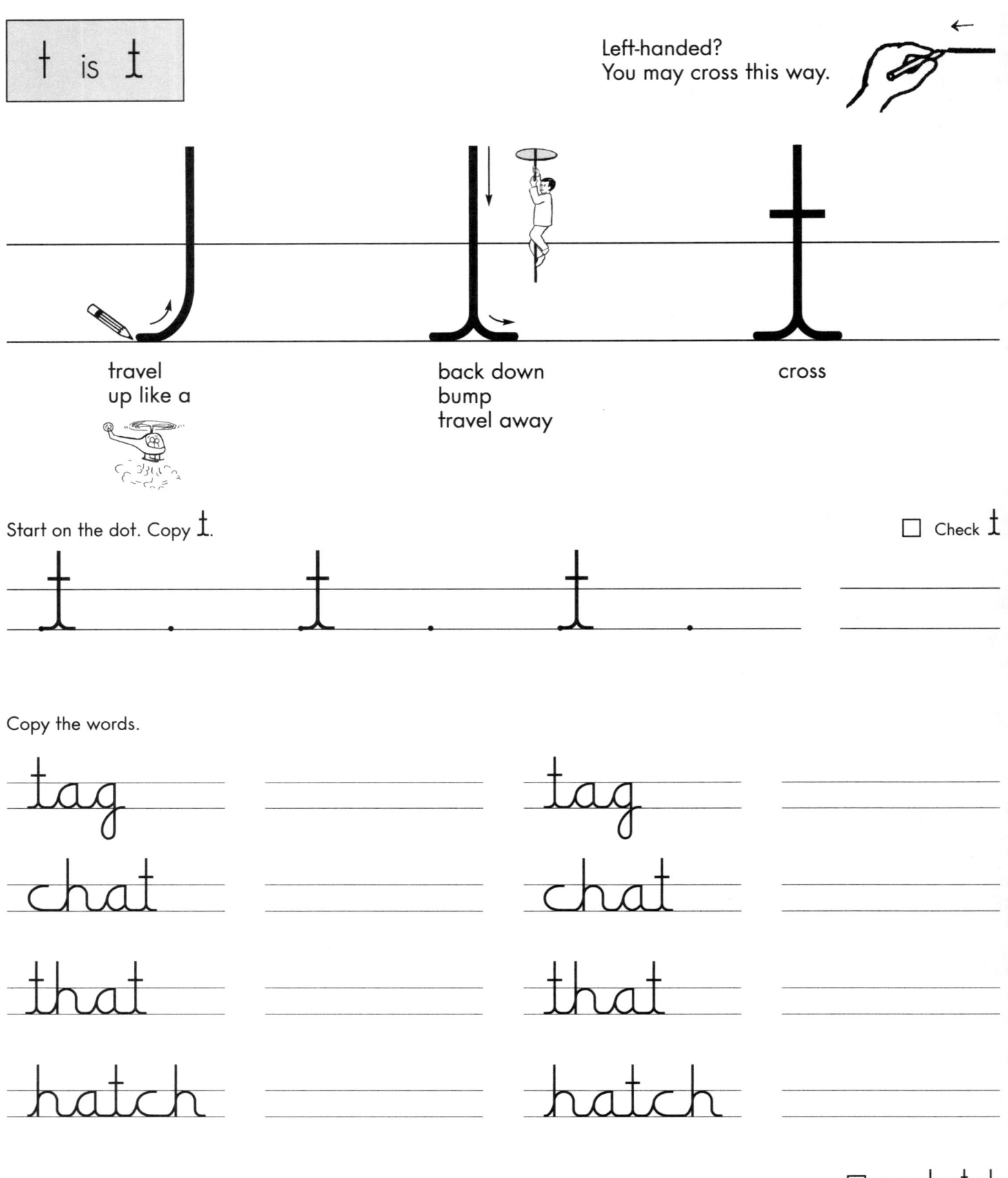

Copy t.

t . t . t . t . t

Add th.

fourth

fif

six

seven

Add atch.

catch

m

p

l

Copy the sentences.

Tad had a cat.

T

That cat had a tag.

T

☐ Check Sentence

✓ Check sentence. Teachers: Help children ✓ their sentence for correct capitalization, word spacing, and ending punctuation.

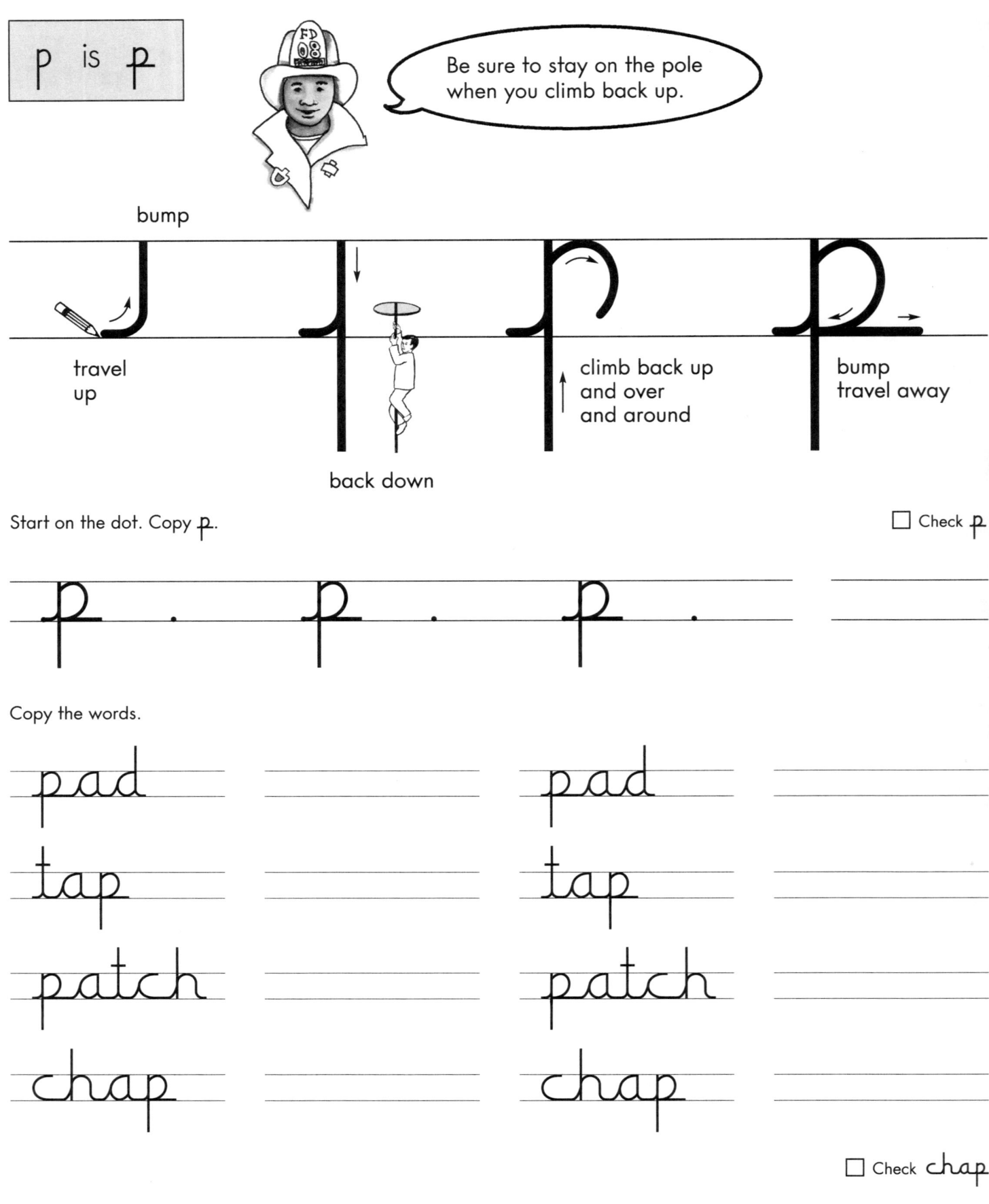

Copy *p*.

p . p . p . p . p

Copy the words.

cap   cap

gap   gap

pat   pat

path   path

Copy the sentences.

Pat had a cap.

P

Papa, catch that.

P

☐ Check Sentence

e is ℓ

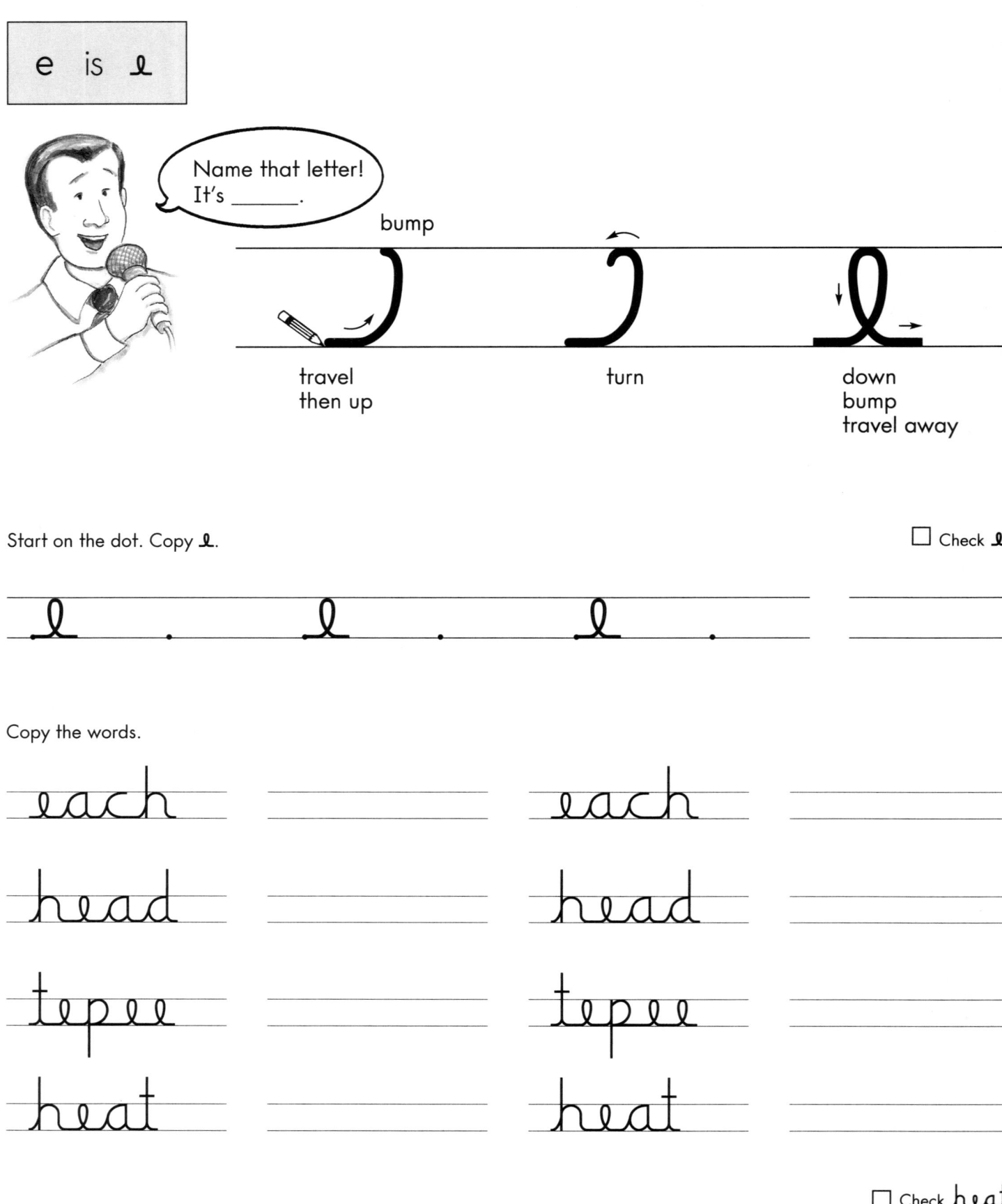

"Name that letter! It's _____."

bump — travel then up — turn — down bump travel away

Start on the dot. Copy ℓ.   ☐ Check ℓ

ℓ .   ℓ .   ℓ .

Copy the words.

each   each
head   head
tepee   tepee
heat   heat

☐ Check heat

20 Cursive Handwriting

Copy *l*.

l . l . l . l . l

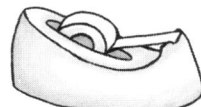

Add *ace*.

race

pl
l
f

Add *ape*.

shape

gr
c
t

Add *eep*.

deep

j
sl
k

Copy the sentences.

Ed ate the peach.

E

Ed patched the cage.

E

☐ Check Sentence

l is l

Name that letter! It's _____.

travel then up   turn   down bump travel away

Start on the dot. Copy l.   ☐ Check l

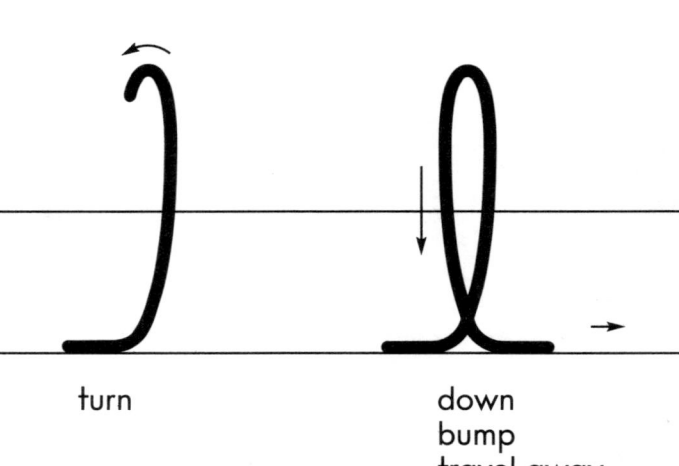

Copy the words.

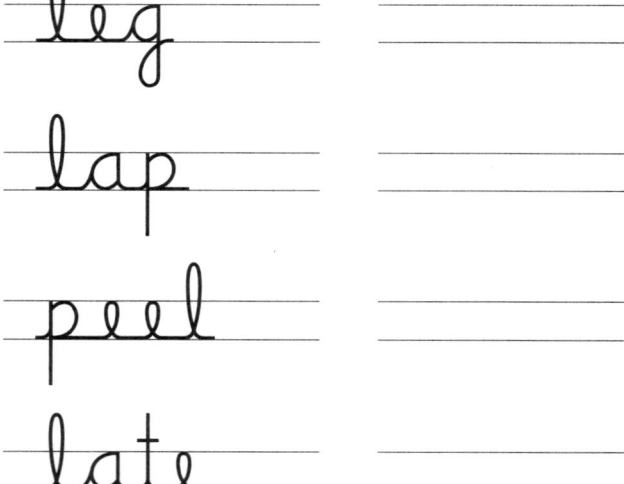

leg   leg

lap   lap

peel   peel

late   late

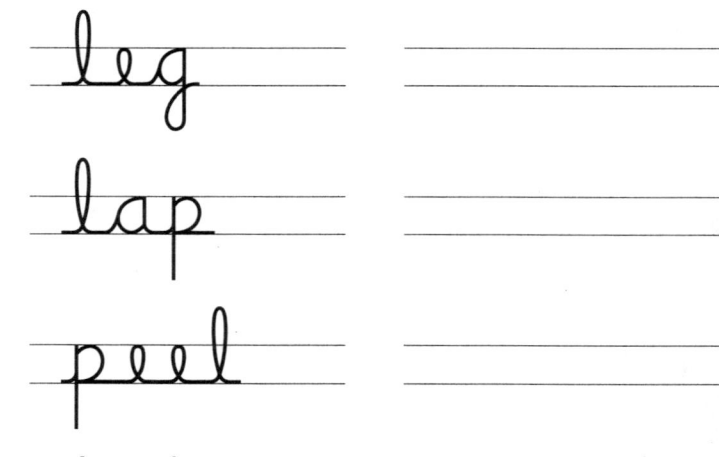

☐ Check late

Copy *l*.

l . l . l . l . l

Add *all*.

hall

m

f

t

Add *ple*.

purple

sam

sim

ap

Add *eel*.

wheel

p

f

h

Copy the sentences.

Leah pet a cat.

L

Lee called a pal.

L

☐ Check Sentence

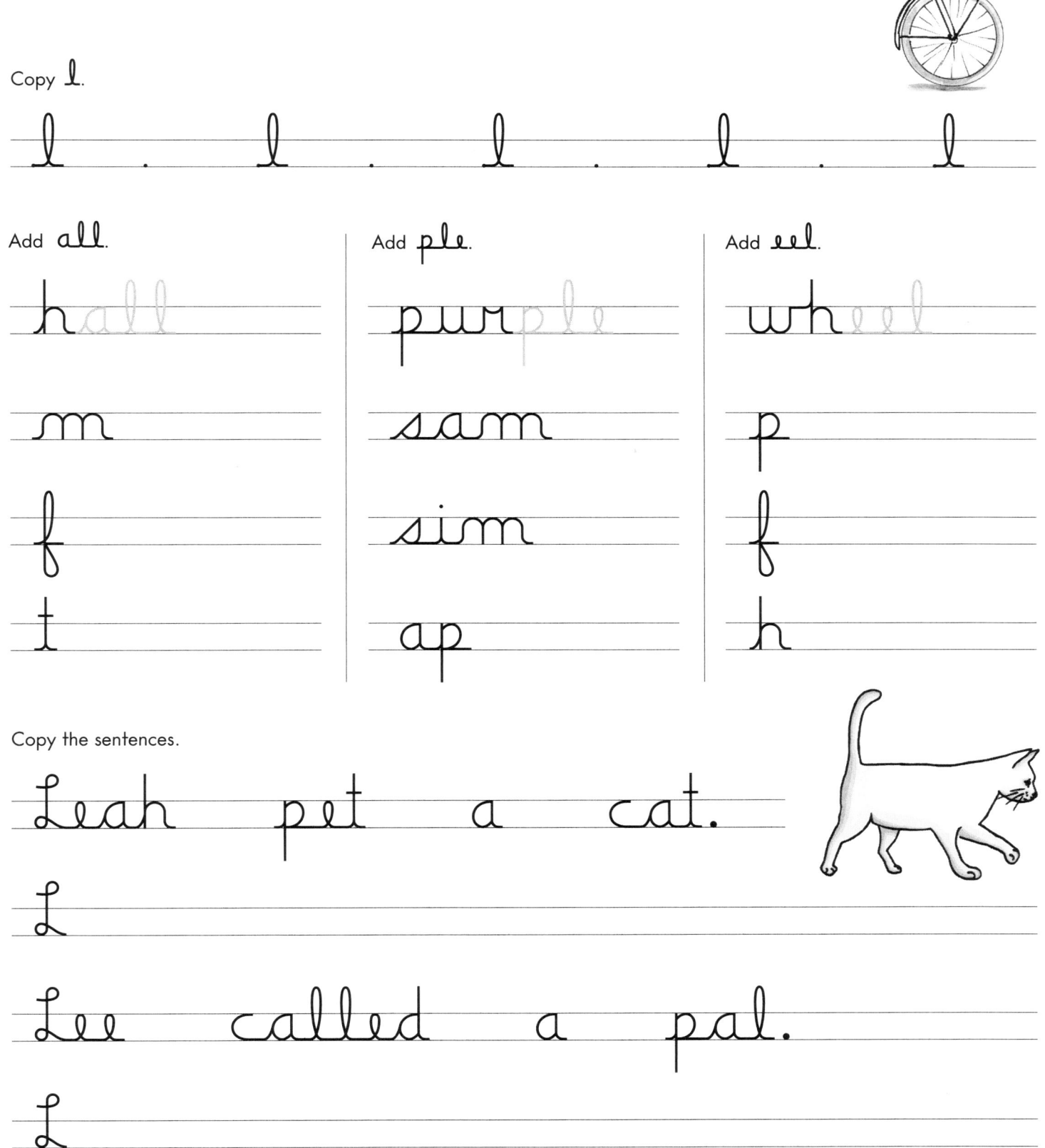

f is f

Make the line as straight as a ruler.

travel then up | turn | down | aim for corner travel away

U-turn

Start on the dot. Copy f. ☐ Check f

Copy the words.

fee   fee
face   face
elf   elf
felt   felt

☐ Check felt

24 Cursive Handwriting © 2022 Learning Without Tears

Copy f.

f f f f f

Add ift.

lift

g

sh

dr

Add fle.

waffle

raf

smif

duf

Copy the sentences.

Fala felt the eel.

F

Face that fact.

F

☐ Check Sentence

Review & Mastery: Cursive to Cursive

a b c d e f g h i j k l m
n o p q r s t u v w x y z

Wait for the teacher to play The Freeze Game.

each - peach

lace - place

hat - that

age - page

all - fall

ate - gate

led - fled

ace - face

| Print to Cursive | Spelling to Cursive |

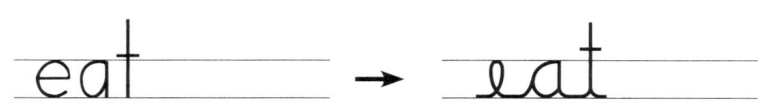

Here are irregular verbs.
Translate the verbs to cursive.

Wait for the teacher to spell the words.
Write the Silly Spelling Words in cursive.

1. eat
2. ate
3. fall
4. fell
5. lead
6. led
7. feel
8. felt

1.
2.
3.
4.
5.
6.
7.
8.

© 2022 Learning Without Tears — See teacher's guide. — Cursive Handwriting **27**

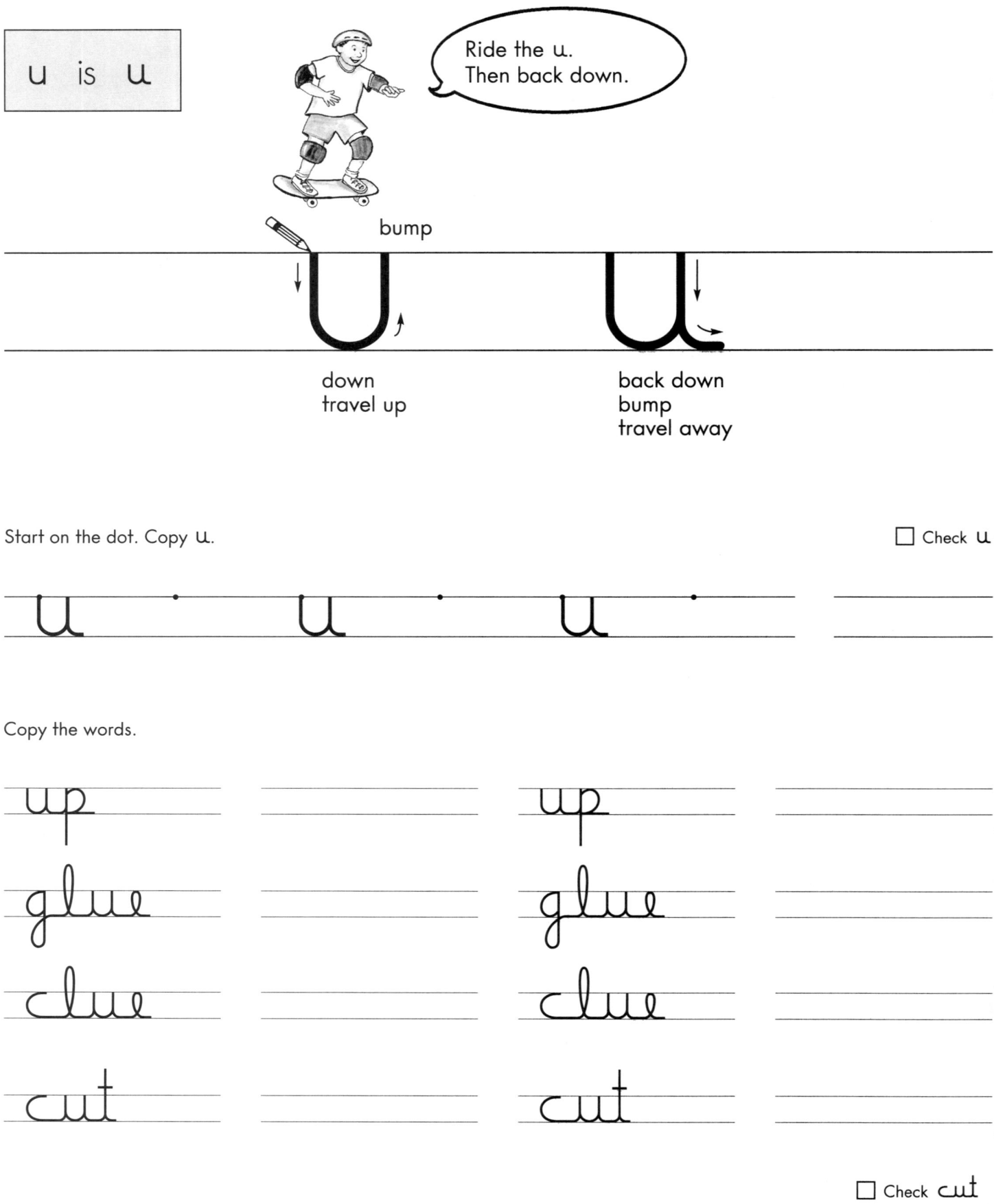

Copy u.

u   u   u   u   u

Add ful.

careful   hope

cheer   help

peace   harm

use   color

Copy the sentences.

Ulla laughed at that.
U

Ulla caught a cap.
U

☐ Check Sentence

y is y

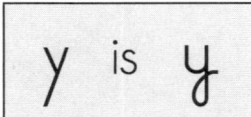

bump
Make the line as straight as a ruler.
down
travel
up
back down
turn
aim for corner
travel away

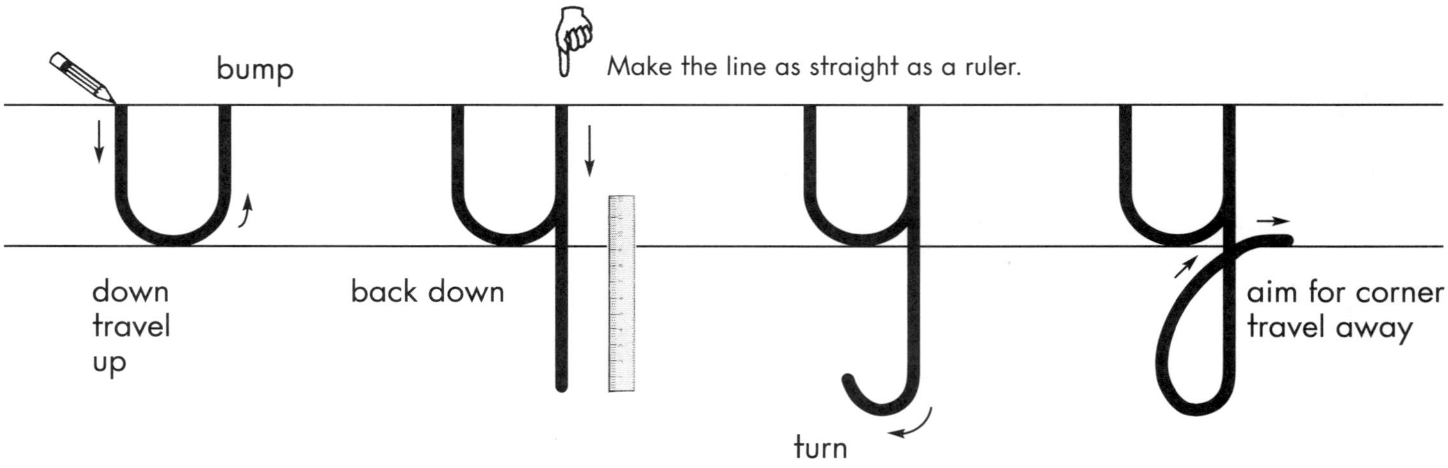

Start on the dot. Copy y.

☐ Check y

y y y

Copy the words.

yell yell

day day

play play

they they

☐ Check they

Copy y.

y   y   y   y   y

Add ty.

twenty   six

thir   seven

for   eigh

fif   nine

Copy the sentences.

Yul yelled, "Help!"

Y   H

Yul played all day.

Y

☐ Check Sentence

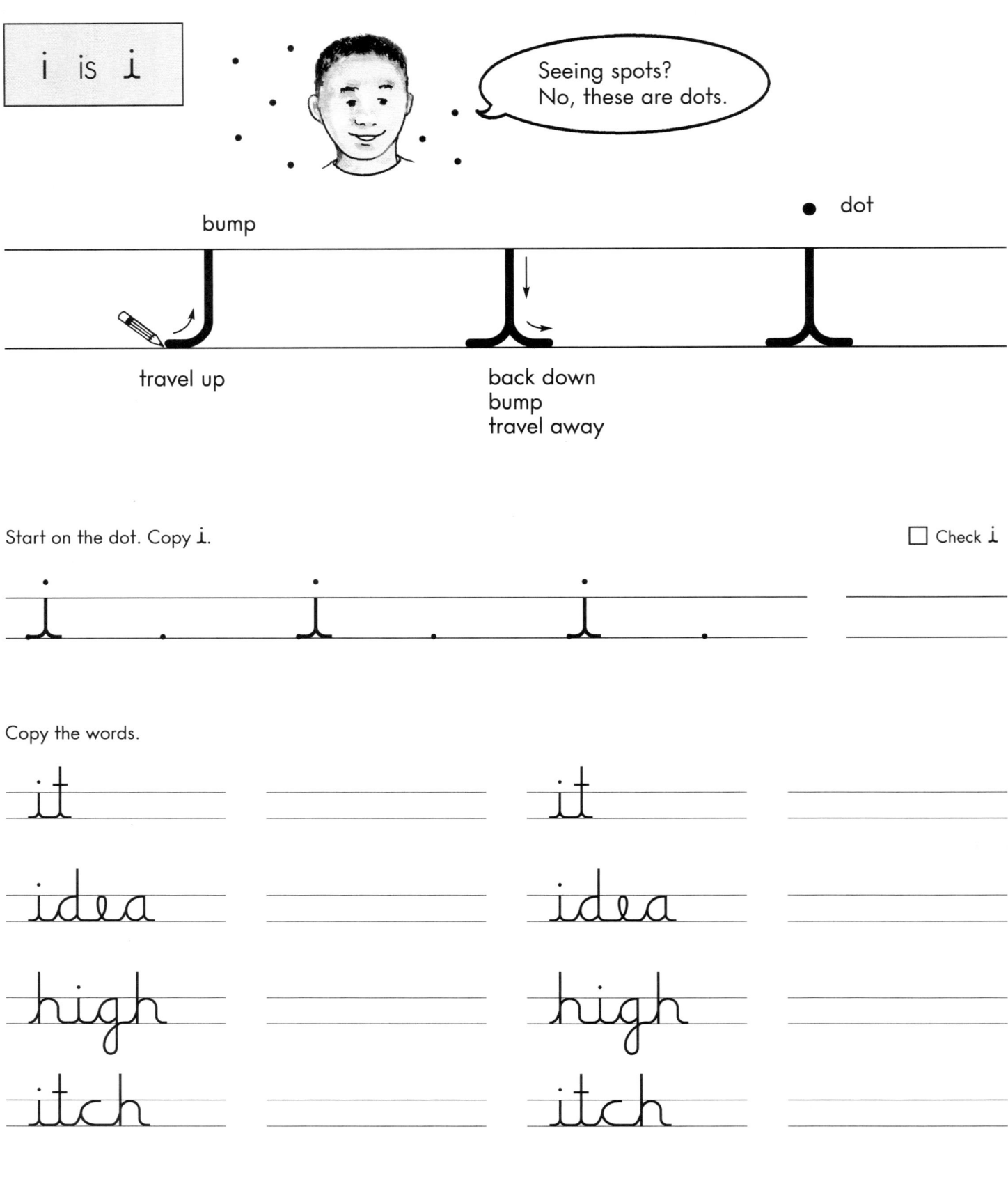

| i is i |

Seeing spots?
No, these are dots.

bump — dot
travel up
back down
bump
travel away

Start on the dot. Copy i.　　　　　　　　　　　　　☐ Check i

Copy the words.

it　　　　　　　it

idea　　　　　idea

high　　　　　high

itch　　　　　itch

☐ Check itch

32　Cursive Handwriting　　　© 2022 Learning Without Tears

Copy i.

i . i . i . i . i

Add ill.

spill
ch
f
thr

Add it.

exit
kn
spl
sk

Add ip.

ship
cl
dr
tr

Copy the sentences.

Ida pitched it high.

I

Ida did a high flip.

I

☐ Check Sentence

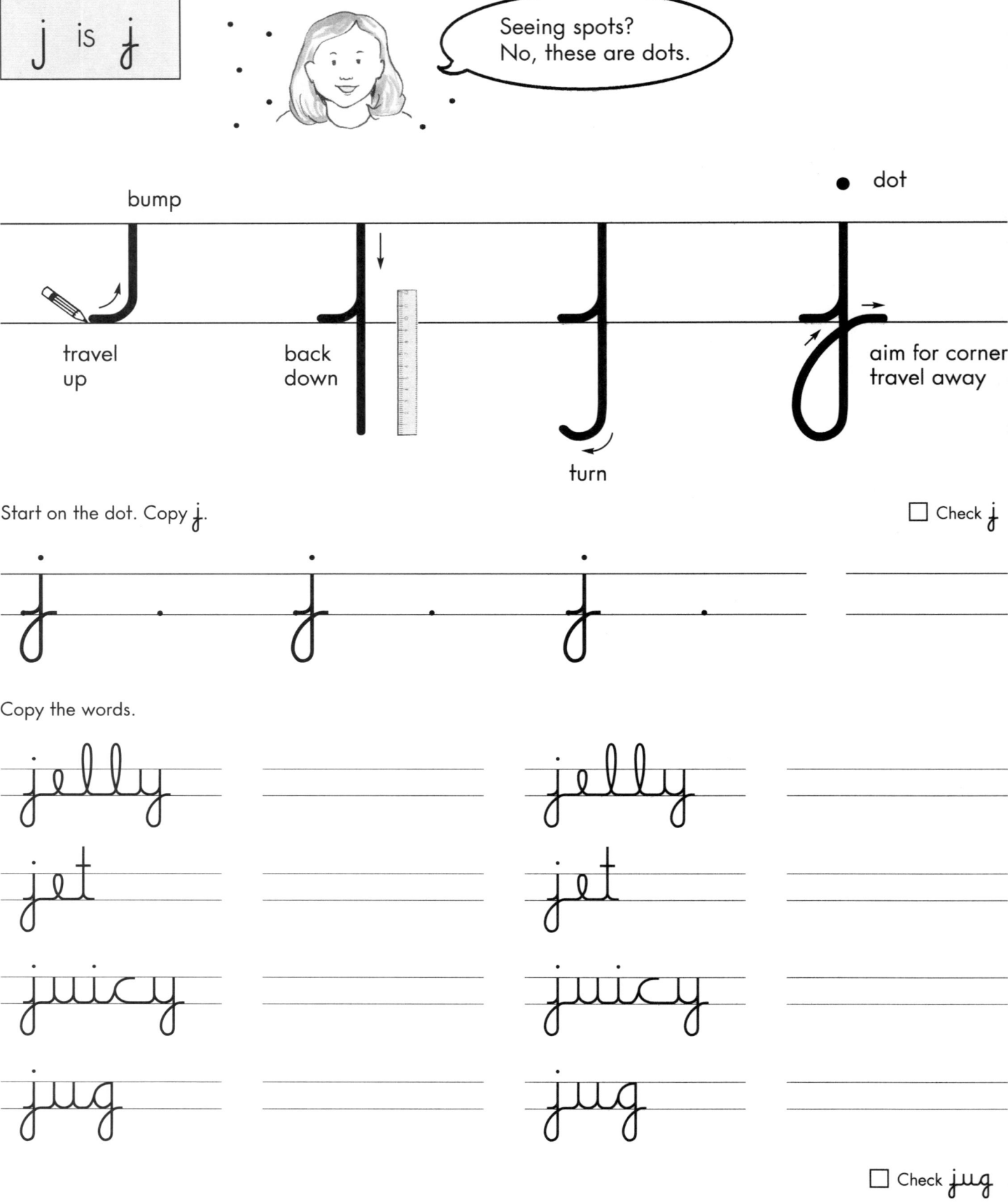

Copy j.

j j j j j

Copy the words.

jay   jay

judge   judge

jeep   jeep

eject   eject

Copy the sentences.

Jade ate a juicy peach.

J

Jaylee juggled.

J

☐ Check Sentence

Review & Mastery: Cursive to Cursive

a b c d e f g h i j k l m
n o p q r s t u v w x y z

Cursive with new letters: u y i j

Wait for the teacher to play The Freeze Game.

jeep - deep

pay - jay

fight - tight

gift - lift

jet - get

field - yield

full - pull

itch - pitch

Print to Cursive	Spelling to Cursive

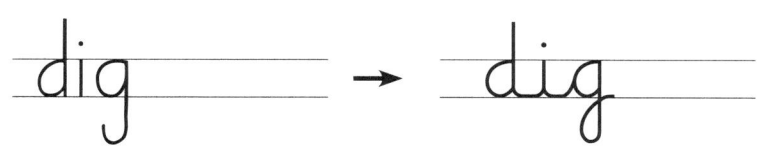

Here are irregular verbs.
Translate print into cursive.

Wait for the teacher to spell the words.
Write the Silly Spelling Words in cursive.

1. dig
2. dug
3. pay
4. paid
5. catch
6. caught
7. light
8. lit

1.
2.
3.
4.
5.
6.
7.
8.

© 2022 Learning Without Tears   See teacher's guide.   *Cursive Handwriting* **37**

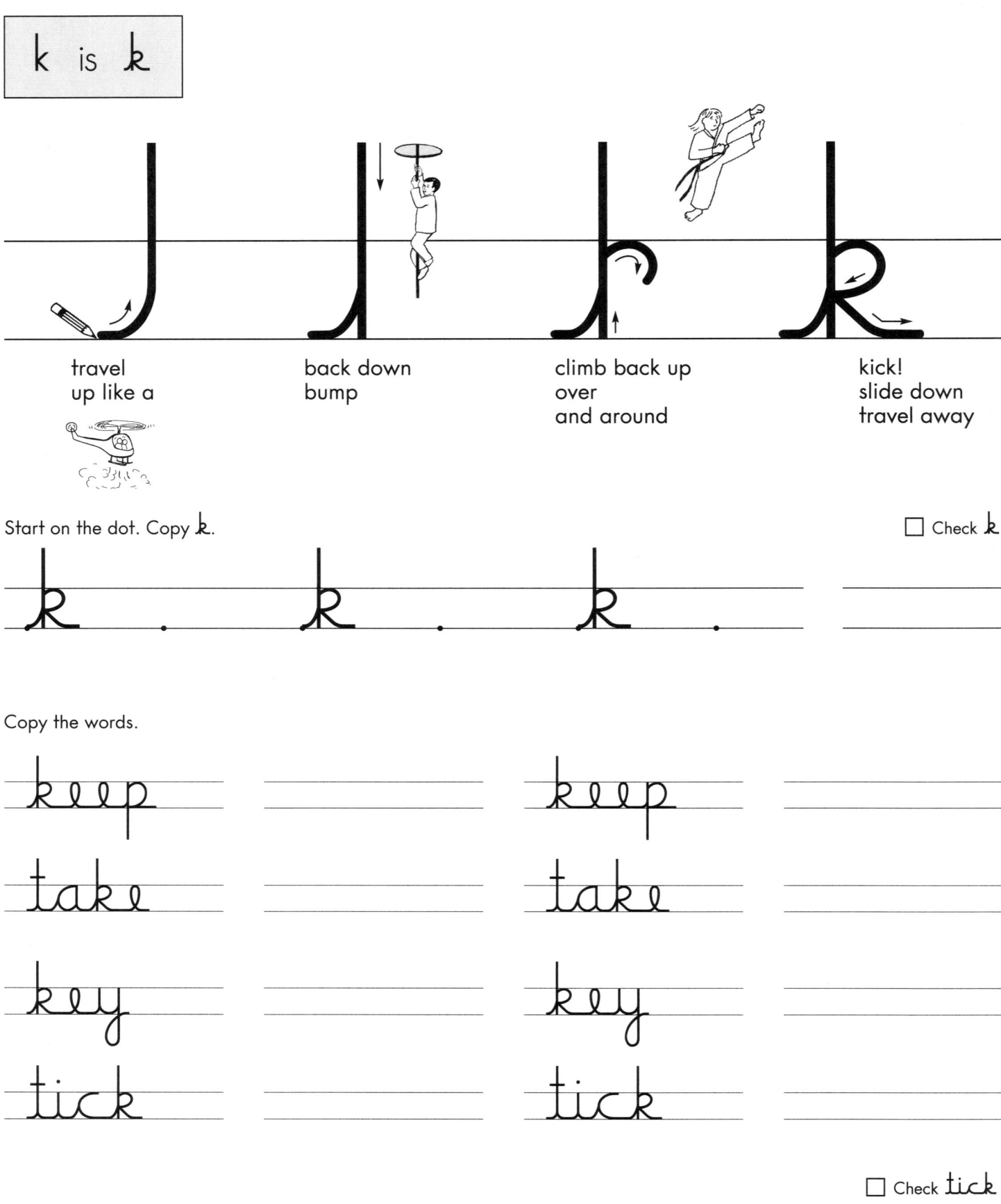

k is k

travel up like a
back down bump
climb back up over and around
kick! slide down travel away

Start on the dot. Copy k. ☐ Check k

k   k   k

Copy the words.

keep   keep
take   take
key   key
tick   tick

☐ Check tick

Copy k.

k . k . k . k . k

Add ick.

trick

br

th

st

Add kle.

pickle

tic

wrin

an

Copy the sentences.

Keith kept the key.
K
Kelly flipped the kayak.
K

☐ Check Sentence

r is ɼ

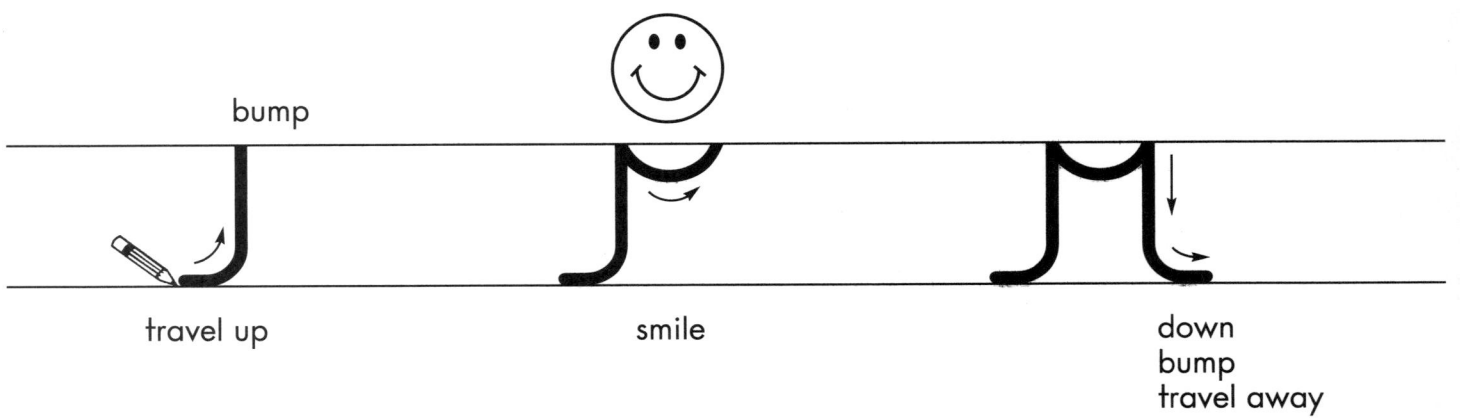

bump — travel up
smile
down bump travel away

Start on the dot. Copy ɼ. ☐ Check ɼ

ɼ .   ɼ .   ɼ .

Copy the words.

race   race

are   are

after   after

their   their

☐ Check their

40 Cursive Handwriting   © 2022 Learning Without Tears

Copy r.

r . r . r . r . r

Add re.
where
ra
ca
sha

Add ear.
Dear
m
y
f

Add ar.
star
c
f
j

Copy the sentences.

Rafael placed third.
R

Rafael raced after her.
R

☐ Check Sentence

Copy *S*.

S . S . S . S . S . S

Add *est*.

tall*est*

short

hard

soft

Add *ist*.

art*ist*

dent

flor

styl

Copy the sentences.

Sarah skates fast.

S

Seth tells tall tales.

S

☐ Check Sentence

Review & Mastery: Cursive to Cursive

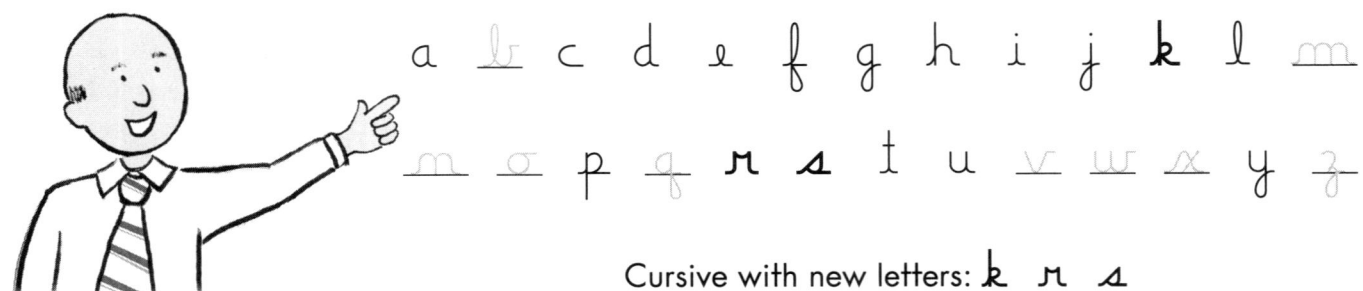

Cursive with new letters: k r s

Wait for the teacher to play The Freeze Game.

she - her

kid - rid

pair - fair

pick - trick

just - rust

ace - aces

rake - take

paid - raid

| Print to Cursive | Spelling to Cursive |

Here are irregular verbs.
Translate print into cursive.

Wait for the teacher to spell the words.
Write the Silly Spelling Words in cursive.

1. sit
2. sat
3. keep
4. kept
5. say
6. said
7. read
8. read

o is o

Now you are ready to learn the Tow Truck Letters. Tow Truck Letters always end with a tow.

Magic c | keep on going | bump | end with a tow

Start on the dot. Copy o. ☐ Check o

Copy the words.

out   out

oar   oar

coat   coat

loud   loud

☐ Check loud

w is ⊍

Tow Truck Letters always end with a tow.

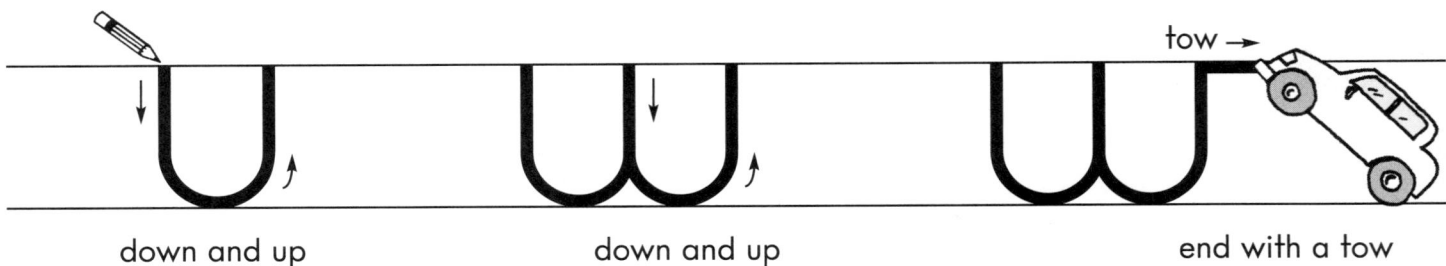

down and up   down and up   end with a tow

Start on the dot. Copy ⊍.   ☐ Check ⊍

Copy the words.

was   was

claw   claw

wash   wash

jaw   jaw

☐ Check jaw

48 Cursive Handwriting   © 2022 Learning Without Tears

Copy w.

Add way.

subway
free
jet
high

Add low.

pillow
hol
yel
fol

Copy the sentences.

Willy saw the walrus.
W

Wait, oh, please wait!
W

☐ Check Sentence

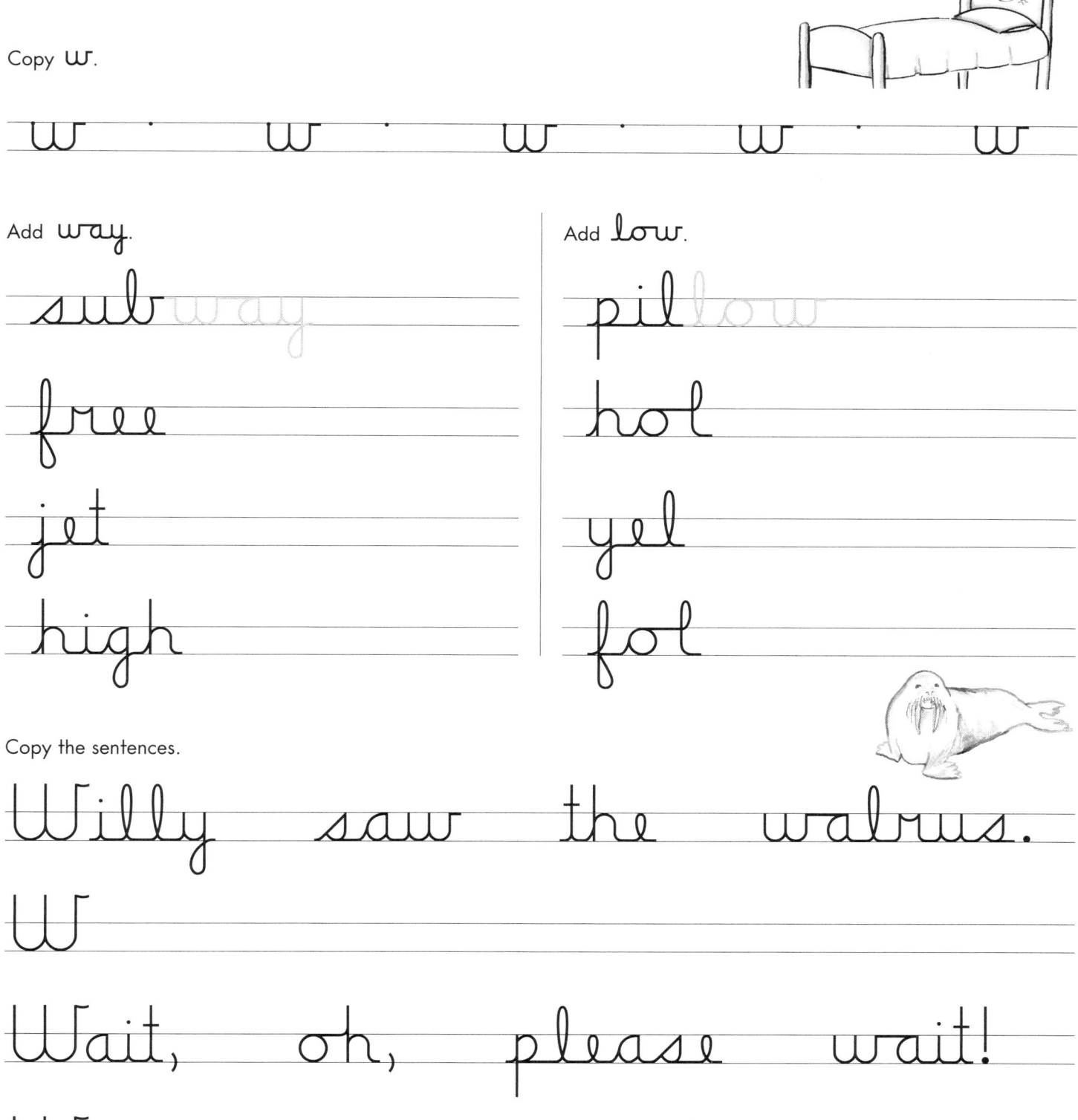

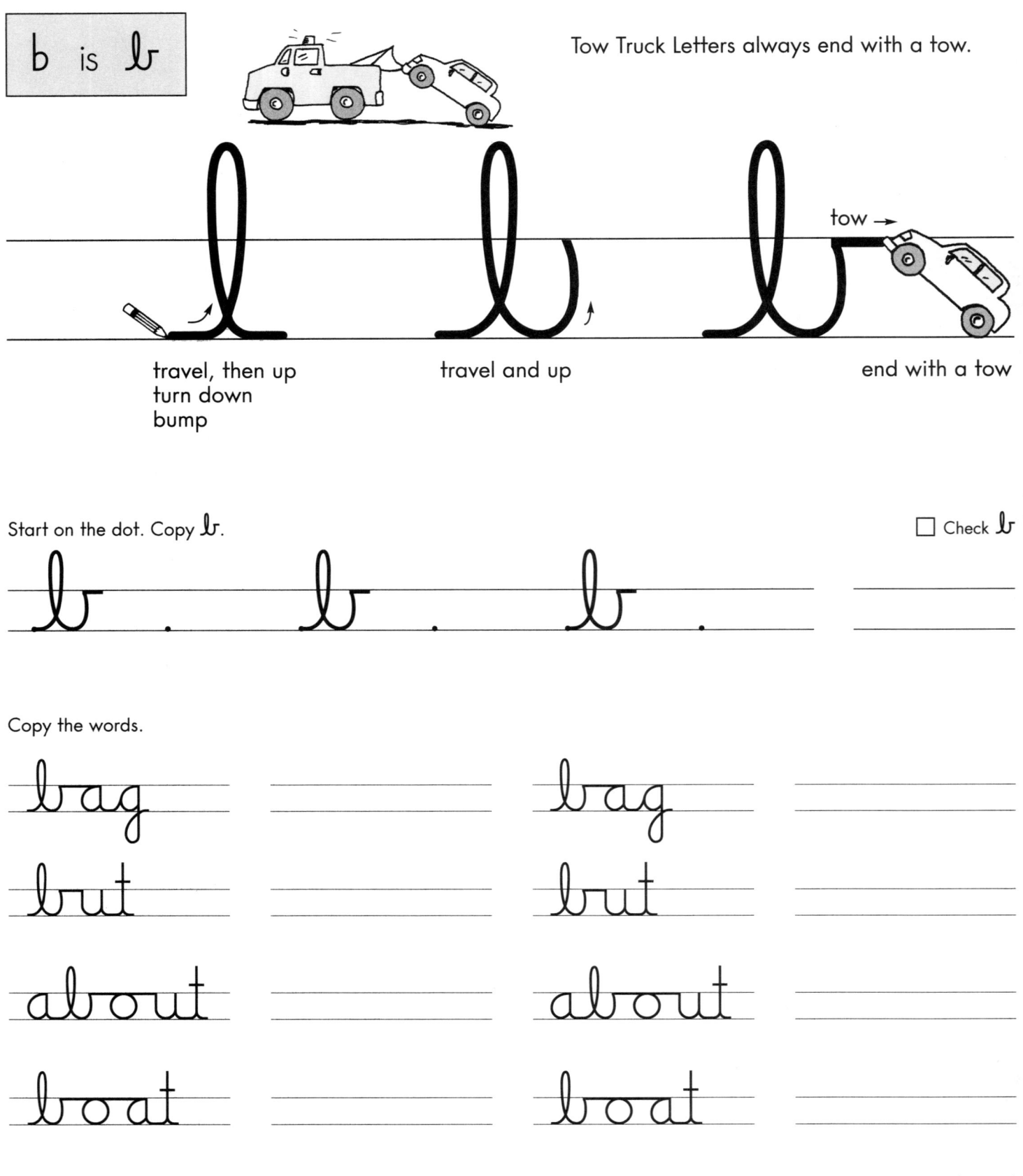

Copy b.

b . b . b . b . b

Copy the words.

baby   baby

crab   crab

base   base

bugs   bugs

Copy the sentences.

Bats fly out at dusk.

B

Bats eat little bugs.

B

☐ Check Sentence

v is v̆

Tow Truck Letters always end with a tow.

slide down · and up · end with a tow

Start on the dot. Copy v̆. ☐ Check v̆

Copy the words.

vow   vow
vast   vast
lava   lava
value   value

☐ Check value

52 Cursive Handwriting © 2022 Learning Without Tears

Copy V.

Copy the words.

vase

vary

vocal

vault

Copy the sentences.

Vultures are bald.

Vipers are reptiles.

☐ Check Sentence

Tricky Connections – after o

 t  k l f

 t  k 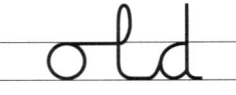 l 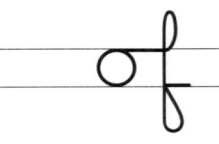 f

Copy the models.

hot   took   old   of

big smile for the tow

 i n l s

 i n e s

Copy the models.

oil   or   toe   lost

Tricky Connections – after ᴡ

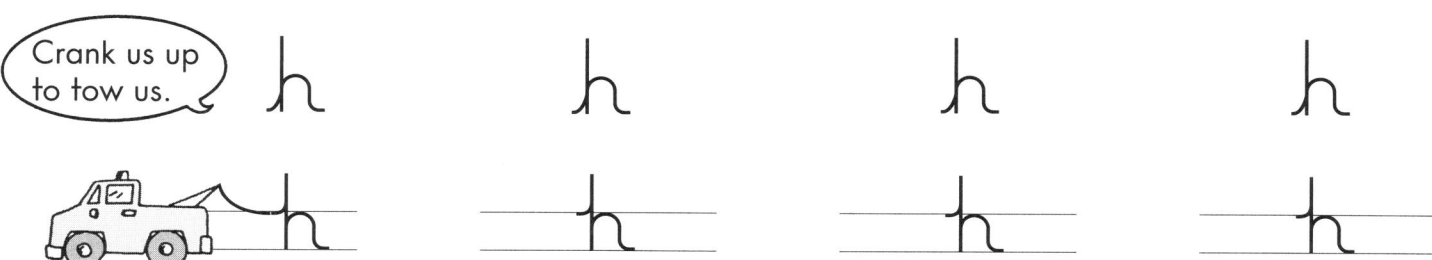

Copy the models.

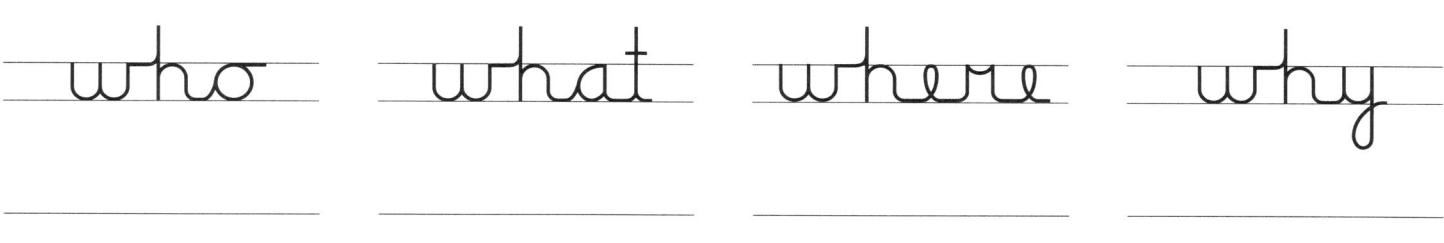

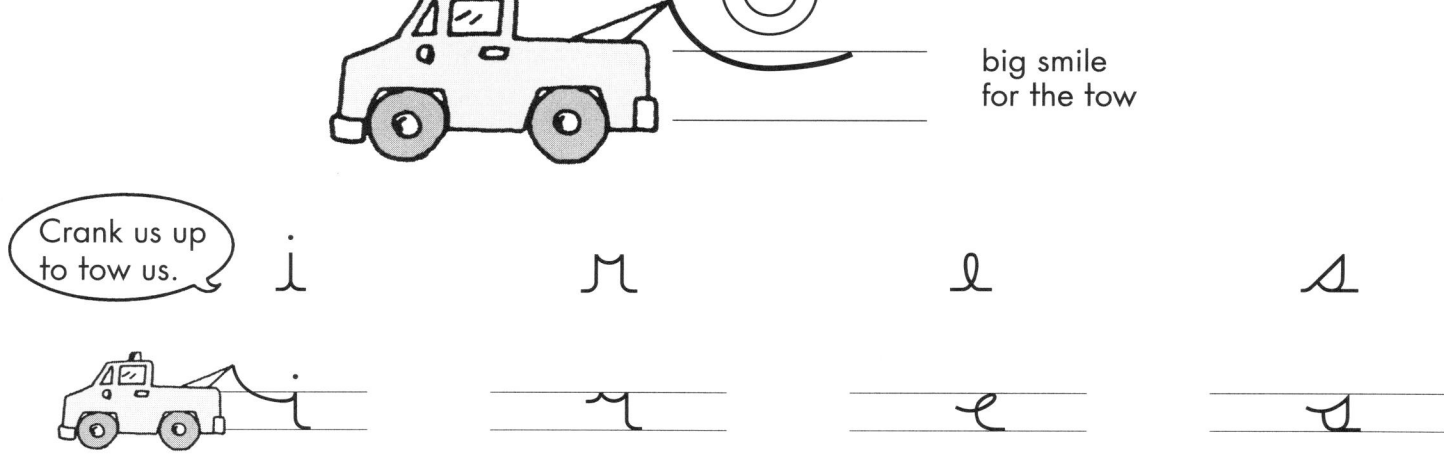

big smile for the tow

Copy the models.

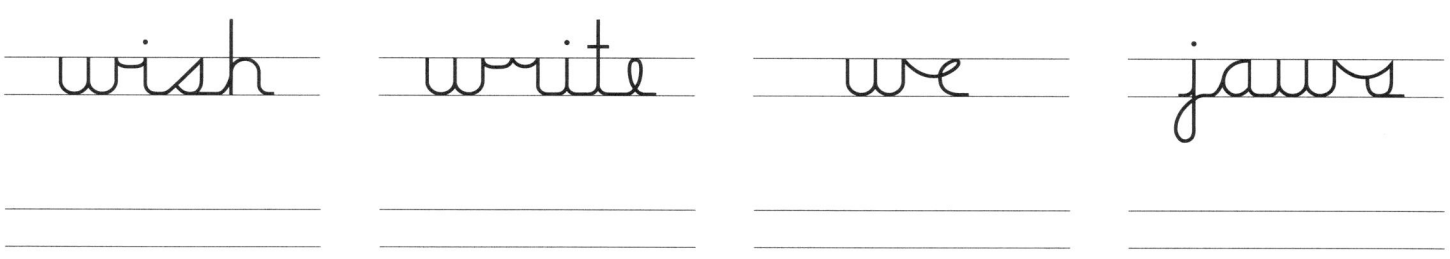

Tricky Connections – after b

 Crank us up to tow us.

l   l   b   b

l   l   b   b

Copy the models.

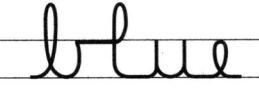

blue   black   rabbit   tabby

big smile for the tow

 Crank us up to tow us.

i   n   e   s

i   n   e   s

Copy the models.

bite   brag   best   tubs

Tricky Connections – after v

big smile for the tow

Crank us up to tow us.

v v v v
v v v v

Copy the models.

very   verb   save   have

Crank us up to tow us.

v v v v
v v v v

Copy the models.

vice   video   view   virus

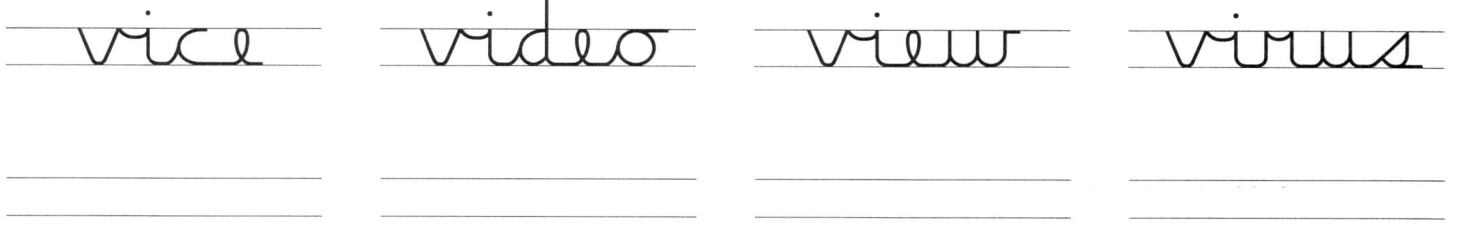

Review & Mastery: Cursive to Cursive

a b c d e f g h i j k l m
n o p q r s t u v w x y z

Cursive with new letters: b o v w

Wait for the teacher to play The Freeze Game.

what - where

for - before

over - ever

avid - avoid

hot - got

best - vest

blue - value

look - took

58 Cursive Handwriting   See teacher's guide.   © 2022 Learning Without Tears

Print to Cursive

Spelling to Cursive

lose → *lose*

Here are irregular verbs.
Translate print into cursive.

Wait for the teacher to spell the words.
Write the Silly Spelling Words in cursive.

1. lose
2. lost
3. give
4. gave
5. write
6. wrote
7. buy
8. bought

1.
2.
3.
4.
5.
6.
7.
8.

m is m

travel
up and over
down

up and over
down

up and over
down
travel away

Start on the dot. Copy m. ☐ Check m

Copy the words.

most   most

same   same

meet   meet

made   made

☐ Check made

Copy m.

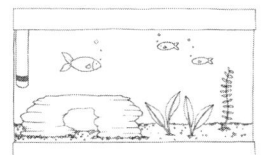

m. m. m. m. m

Add ium.

calcium   aquar

uran   stad

sod   med

lith   gymnas

Copy the sentences.

Some mammals swim.

S

Mice are mammals.

M

☐ Check Sentence

n is m

travel
up and over
down

up and over
down
travel away

Start on the dot. Copy m. ☐ Check m

m.   m.   m.

Copy the words.

not   not

and   and

near   near

mail   mail

☐ Check mail

Copy m.

m . m . m . m . m

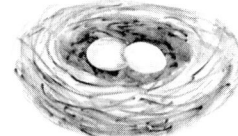

Copy the words.

nest   nest

nose   nose

even   even

name   name

Copy the sentences.

Saturn has many rings.

S

Neptune is a planet.

N

☐ Check Sentence

Cursive Handwriting **63**

SPECIAL SITUATION

After a Tow Truck Letter, use **printed** m.

Start on the dot. Copy m.　　　　　　　　　　☐ Check m

come

from

home

some

☐ Check some

SPECIAL SITUATION

After a Tow Truck Letter, use **printed** n.

Start on the dot. Copy n. ☐ Check n

Copy the words.

on

own

only

none

☐ Check none

Cursive Handwriting **65**

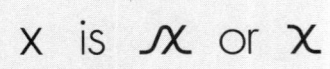 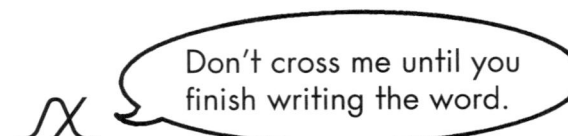

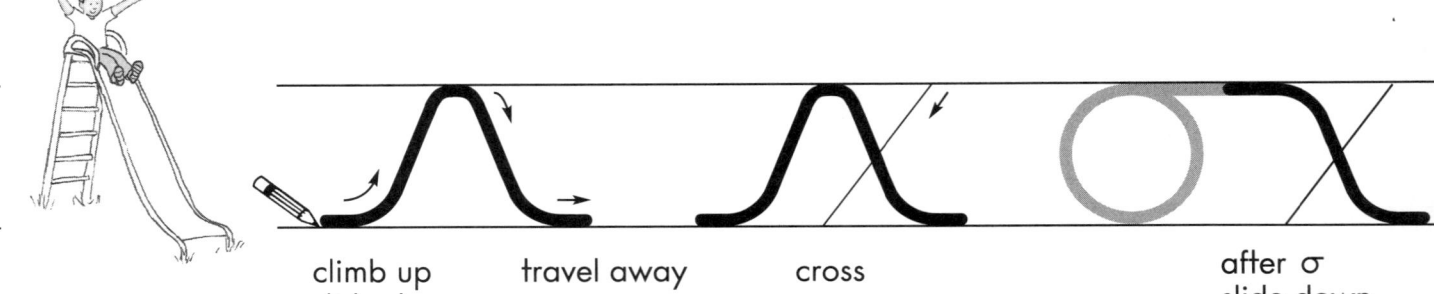

Start on the dot. Copy 𝓍. ☐ Check 𝓍

Copy the words.

exit   exit

sixty   sixty

tax   tax

exam   exam

☐ Check exam

Copy *x* and *X*.

x . x . x . x . x

Add *ix*.

mix

f

s

m

Add *ox*.

fox

b

phl

l

Copy the sentences.

X-rays show bones.

X

Xavier took an exam.

X

☐ Check Sentence

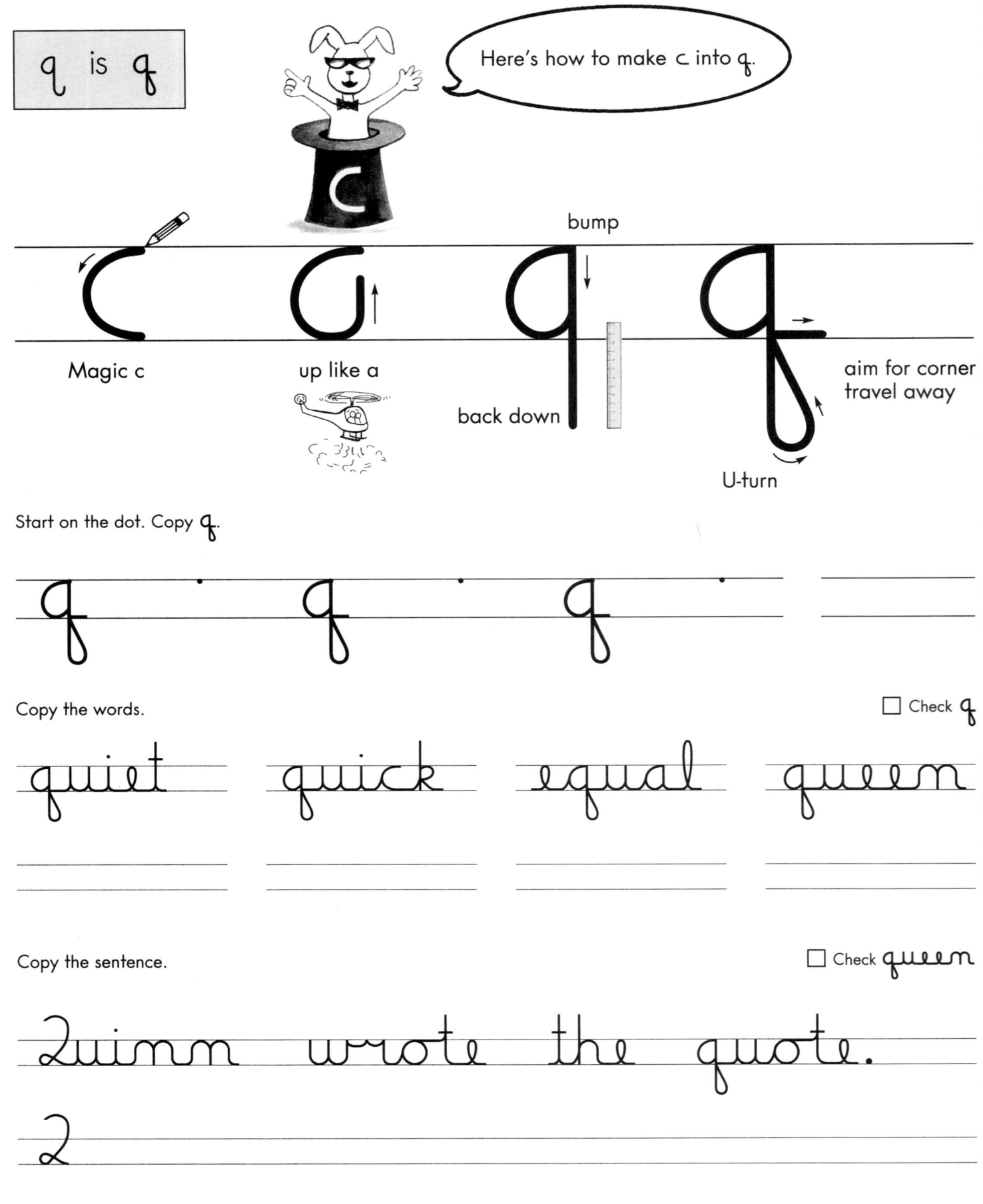

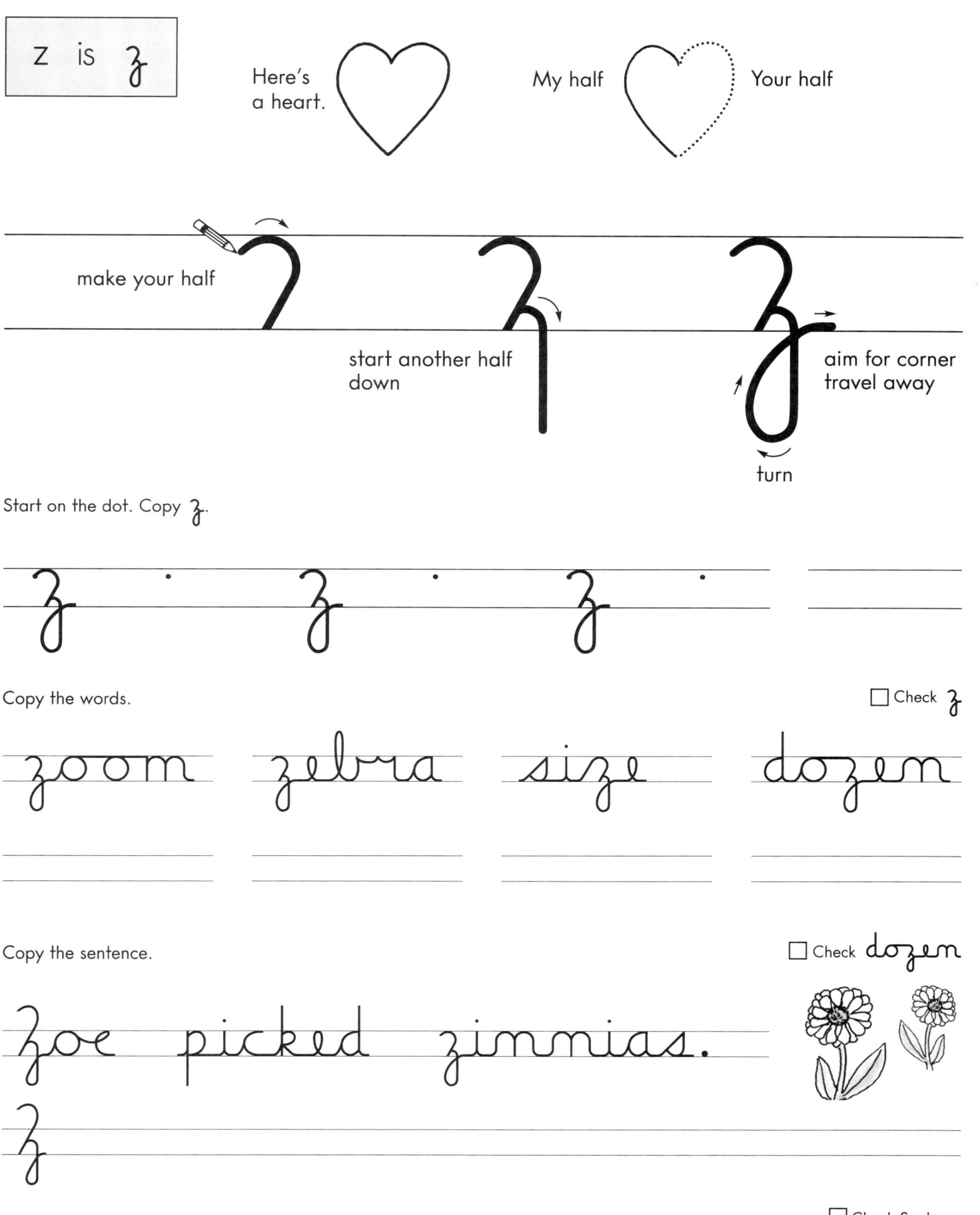

Review & Mastery: Cursive to Cursive

a b c d e f g h i j k l m
n o p q r s t u v w x y z

Cursive with new letters: m n q x z

Wait for the teacher to play The Freeze Game.

came - same

come - some

win - mine

won - none

six - fix

box - fox

quit - quiz

size - prize

| Print to Cursive | Spelling to Cursive |

Here are the irregular verbs.
Translate print into cursive.

Wait for the teacher to spell the words.
Write the Silly Spelling Words in cursive.

1. make
2. made
3. know
4. knew
5. freeze
6. froze
7. quit
8. quit

1.
2.
3.
4.
5.
6.
7.
8.

Trace the steps.　　　Trace the first word. Copy the sentences.

Magic C　up　back down

A asked, "Are you asleep?"

ready down　up around　around again

Bob backpacked in Brazil.

Magic C

Cindy called Cousin Carl.

down small turn　flip over　curve up end

Dan drove on Delo Dr.

c in the air　c again

Ed enjoyed Europe.

ready down　J-turn　cross

Fiona flew on Friday.

72　Cursive Handwriting　© 2022 Learning Without Tears

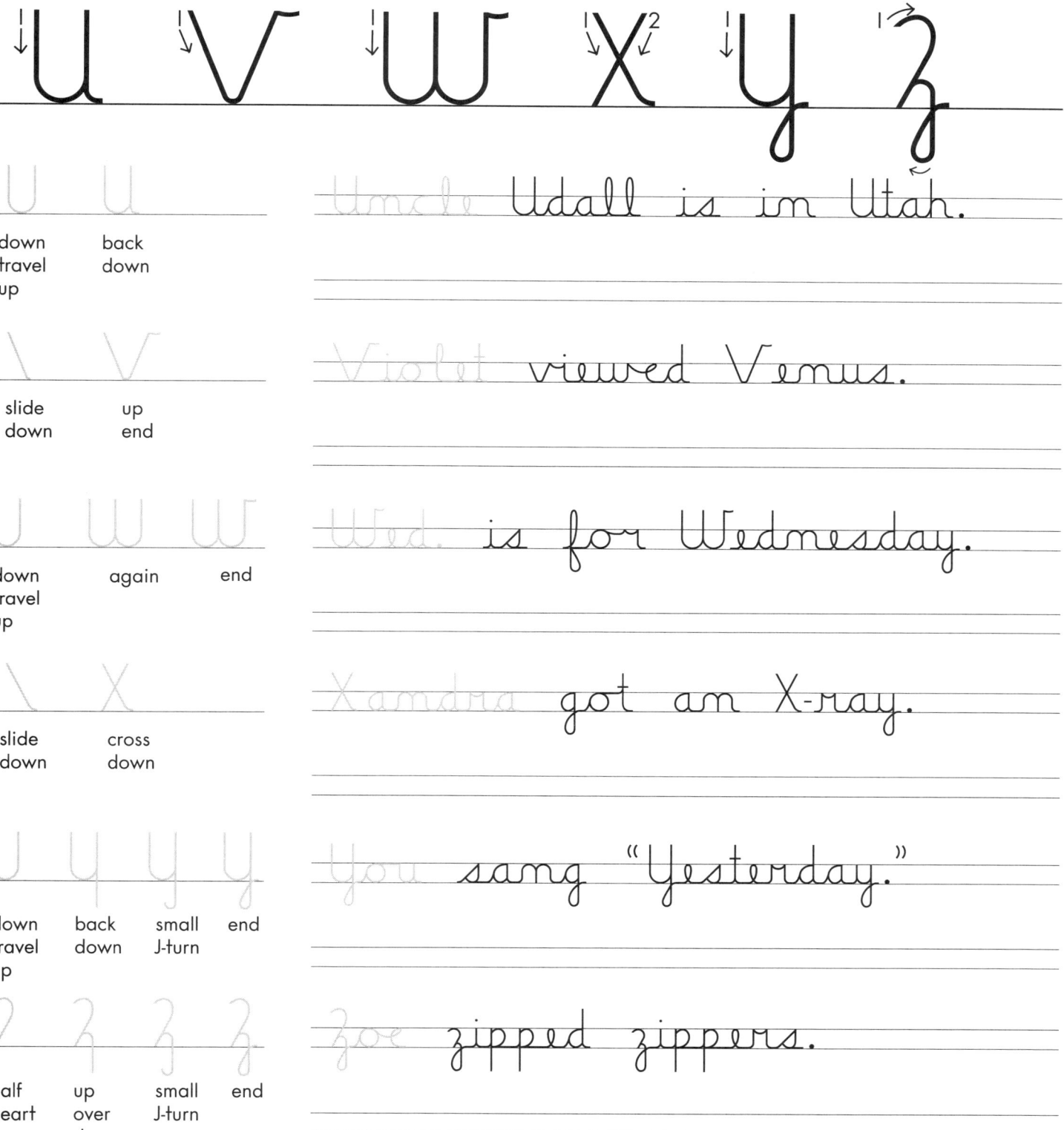

CAPITAL CONNECTIONS

These capitals connect. Copy the capitals and connect to the lowercase letter.

Aa   Cc   Ee   Jj   Kk   Ll   Mm

Nn   Qq   Rr   Uu   Yy   Zz

These capitals DO NOT connect. Copy.

Bb   Dd   Ff   Gg   Hh   Ii   Oo

Pp   Ss   Tt   Vv   Ww   Xx

CAPITAL REVIEW

Translate the capitals into cursive.

A   B   C   D   E   F   G   H

I   J   K   L   M   N   O   P   Q

R   S   T   U   V   W   X   Y   Z

POEM

You're or Your?

If you're (you are) going for a run,

You're, the contraction, is the one,

But if you have lost your shoes,

Possessive your is what to use.

Change print to cursive.

We're racing for our team.

WORDS

Use Greek and Latin to figure out big words.

Copy.
PREFIXES

pre- = before   preview

auto- = self   autograph

WORD ROOTS

aqua = water   aquarium

graph = writing   geography

geo, terra = earth   territory

SUFFIXES

-arium = place for   terrarium

-ology = study of   geology

PARAGRAPH

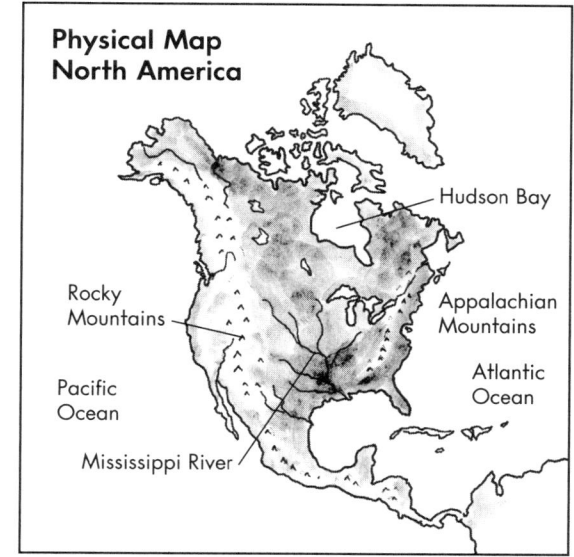

POLITICAL MAPS
Land and water outlines
Countries – names and borders

PHYSICAL MAPS
Land – terrain: mountains, deserts, flat lands
Water features – rivers, lakes

Use the information. Complete the body of the paragraph.

Look at maps. All maps are flat.

Political maps show

Physical maps show

Maps show different things.

PUNCTUATION

Copy the punctuation marks.

. . . . Periods

? ? ? Question marks

! ! ! Exclamation points

DATES
Here are the birth dates of important people.
Some of them are in this book. Copy the dates.

Jan. 11, 1755   Feb. 15, 1820   Mar. 4, 1877

Apr. 25, 1917   May 3, 1919   June 5, 1899

July 29, 1877   Aug. 5, 1930   Sept. 26, 1898

Oct. 2, 1869   Nov. 30, 1835   Dec. 25, 1821

GREETINGS & CLOSINGS
Copy. ☐ Check Word

Dear   Sincerely,   Thank you,   Love,

FRIENDLY LETTER

Write a thank you letter. Organize your letter like this.

Date
Month Day, Year

Greeting
Dear _____ ,

Body
Say, "thank you" and explain how much you appreciate the gift or help. Mention what it is or what they did. Add details to make it more personal.

Closing
Sincerely, Thank you, or Love,

Signature

Use a comma:
1. After the day of the month
2. After the greeting
3. After the closing

WORDS

astronomer   author   inventor   pianist   magician   philosopher   jazz singer

These are suffixes for people: – er, – or, – ist, – ian.

Copy.

– er: astronomer, diver, teacher

– or: author, doctor, inventor

– ist: pianist, dentist, motorist

– ian: magician, physician, optician

– er: philosopher, jazz singer

– ist: scientist, artist

PARAGRAPH

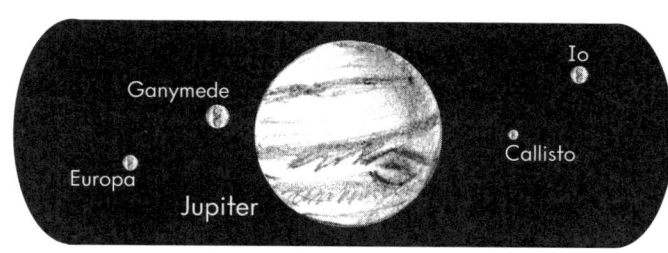

Look at the night sky. If it's clear, you'll see countless stars, a few planets, and one moon. Galileo, an astronomer, was the first to see more moons. In 1609, he made a telescope strong enough to see four of Jupiter's moons.

SYMBOLS

1. exclamation
2. at
3. number
4. dollar
5. percent

6. caret
7. and
8. asterisk
9. open parenthesis
0. close parenthesis

Write the symbol name in cursive.

! _____   ^ _____

@ _____   & _____

_____   * _____

$ _____   (_____

% _____   ) _____

Cursive Handwriting

LETTERS

knack knife knew knees

wreck wrap write wrist

climb lamb crumb thumb

Write sentences with some of the words.

SENTENCES

Capitalize titles like: Mr., Dr., Ms., Miss, Mrs.
Capitalize the first, last, and important words in book, movie, and song titles.

CAPITALIZE: Finish the sentences about yourself.

Schools — My school is _____.

Titles, names — My teacher is _____.

Book titles — I read _____.

Movie titles — I saw _____.

Song titles — I can sing _____.

Cities, towns — I live in _____.

Rivers, lakes, oceans — The closest water is _____.

First word of a quote — I said, " _____."

☐ Check Sentence

NAMES
Copy the names.

- Born Sept. 26, 1898
- Pianist and composer
- Wrote "Rhapsody in Blue"

George Gershwin

- Born April 29, 1899
- Composer, pianist, and bandleader
- Wrote "It Don't Mean a Thing"

Duke Ellington

- Born April 25, 1917
- Jazz singer and "First Lady of Song"
- Sang "I've Got Rhythm"

Ella Fitzgerald

- Born May 3, 1919
- Folk singer and composer
- Wrote "If I Had a Hammer"

Pete Seeger

Write about one of these musicians or another favorite of yours.

PARAGRAPH

TROPICAL RAINFOREST

EMERGENT LAYER: parrots, butterflies

CANOPY: monkeys, toucans

UNDERSTORY: sloths, snakes, lizards

FOREST FLOOR: insects, jaguars, anteaters, frogs

Finish the sentences.

A tropical rainforest bursts with life. At the top,

Just below

The understory

The floor is home to

SENTENCES

CAPITALIZE: Finish the sentences about yourself.

Initials — My initials are ___. ___. ___.

Names — My name is ___.

Days — Today is ___.

Months — My birthday is in ___.

Languages — I speak ___.

Holidays — My favorite holiday is ___.

Names — I admire ___.

Places — I would like to visit ___.

☐ Check Sentence

PARAGRAPH

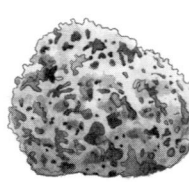
sponge

Garret Augustus Morgan, Sr.
born March 4, 1877
inventor of safety hood device
1916 Lake Erie tunnel explosion

Men were trapped in the smoky tunnel. Firemen couldn't go in. Then, Garret put on his safety hood invention. A wet sponge cooled and cleaned the air. He could breathe! He saved two lives.

☐ Check Sentences

WORDS

Fill in the blanks to make compound words.

sun: _sun_ + _light_ = _sunlight_

rain: _____ + _bow_ = _____

fire: _____ + _fly_ = _____

lantern: _____ + _fish_ = _____

bed: _____ + _time_ = _____

SIX SYL – LA – BLE WORD

bi – o – lu – mi – nes – cent

bio   biolumi   bioluminescent

PARAGRAPH

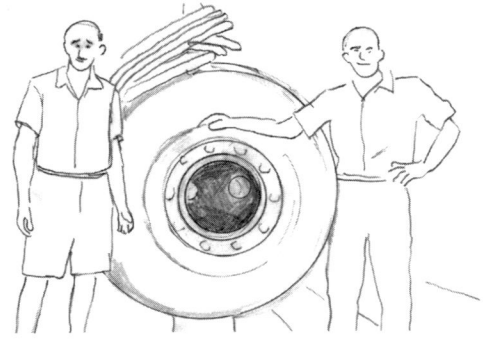

Bathysphere
- Strong, steel hollow ball
- Tied to ship, lowered and raised
- Oxygen hoses, phone, and electric cables
- 1930–1934 near Bermuda

Bathysphere

William Beebe, born July 25, 1877
- Planned dive to deep ocean (Abyss)
- Marine biologist, famous scientist
- First to see the Abyss with Barton
- Described bioluminescent creatures

Otis Barton, born June 5, 1899
- Heard about Beebe's plan
- Engineer with design ideas
- Inventor of Bathysphere
- Made deepest dive with Beebe

Finish the paragraph.

Beebe and Barton were a team.

PARAGRAPH

What's in the midnight zone, the deep, dark ocean? There's a light show! Bioluminescent animals glow and blink.

SENTENCES

Always do right.

Mark Twain
- Born Nov. 30, 1835

Translate the quotations into cursive.

Mark Twain said, "Always do right."

Independence is happiness.

Susan B. Anthony
- Born Feb. 15, 1820

学而时习之，不亦说乎.

To learn and to practice is a joy.

Confucius
- Born Sept. 28, 551 BCE

☐ Check Sentence